Contents

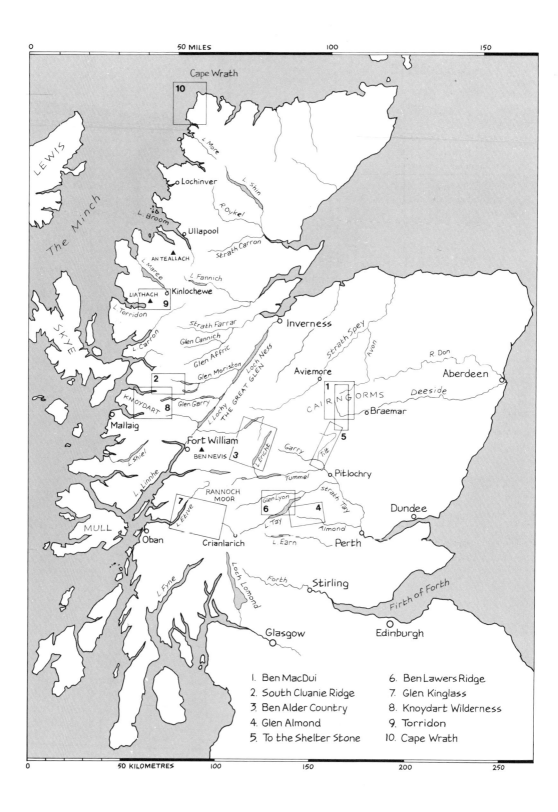

0   50 MILES   100   150

Cape Wrath

10

LEWIS

The Minch

o Lochinver

L. More

L. Shin

R. Oykel

L. Broom

o Ullapool

Strath Carron

▲ AN TEALLACH

L. Maree

L. Fannich

LIATHACH

9

o Kinlochewe

L. Torridon

SKYE

Strath Farrar

Glen Cannich

Inverness

Strath Spey

Glen Affric

Avon

R. Don

Glen Moriston

Loch Ness

Aviemore

Aberdeen

L. Carron

2

THE GREAT GLEN

CAIRNGORMS

Deeside

KNOYDART

8

Glen Garry

L. Lochy

o Braemar

Mallaig

1

5

Fort William

L. Eriche

Garry

Tilt

▲ BEN NEVIS

3

Tummel

o Pitlochry

L. Shiel

RANNOCH MOOR

Strath Tay

L. Linnhe

7

Glen Lyon

4

Dundee

L. Etive

6

MULL

L. Tay

Almond

Oban

Crianlarich

L. Earn

Perth

Loch Lomond

Forth

Stirling

L. Fyne

Firth of Forth

Glasgow

Edinburgh

1. Ben MacDui   6. Ben Lawers Ridge
2. South Cluanie Ridge   7. Glen Kinglass
3. Ben Alder Country   8. Knoydart Wilderness
4. Glen Almond   9. Torridon
5. To the Shelter Stone   10. Cape Wrath

0   50 KILOMETRES   100   150   200   250

ROUTE GUIDE

Route	Duration (Days)	Technical Difficulty	Distance km (miles)	Elevation m (ft)	Maps
1. The Grey Man of Ben MacDui	4	moderate	52 (32)	1,950 (6,400)	36 and 43 OL3
2. Skywalking the South Cluanie Ridge	1–3	difficult	22.5 (14)	1,950 (6,400)	33
3. Training to Ski – Ben Alder Country	4	moderate/ difficult	67 (42)	1,930 (6,300)	42 and 41
4. Star-gazing In Glen Almond	1–2	easy	22 (13½)	420 (1,400)	52
5. 30 Miles to the Shelter Stone	3–4	easy/ moderate	73 (46)	1,020 (3,350)	43 and 36
6. Ben Lawers Walk – Alpine Flora and Ice-Age Flo	1–3	moderate/ difficult	20 (12½)	2,040 (6,700)	51
7. Glen Kinglass and the Anatomy of a Depression	2	easy	43 (27)	520 (1,700)	50
8. Knoydart Wilderness	4–5	difficult	60 (37½)	2,600 (8,530)	33
9. Torridon by Night	1–2	difficult	22 (13½)	1,400 (4,590)	OL8
10. Midsummer at Cape Wrath	3	moderate	38 (24)	960 (3,150)	9

Note: Technical difficulty is given for the walks as experienced by the author. Accordingly, walkers doing the walks in different seasons from those described (or under significantly different weather conditions) should modify the subjective ratings given above.

Acknowledgements

I would like to express my sincere thanks to the Department of Physical Education, Edinburgh University, for tolerating my haphazard timetable and allowing me sufficient time to complete the active part of this book's research. I am grateful for the assistance of Dennis Rewt and Colin Cruickshank for advice on technical matters and Ian Campbell and Jeff McCarthy for proof-reading the manuscript. Gaelic translations appearing in the index are by Donald Meek, to whom I owe special thanks. Photographic advice from Steve Senio and Ian Underwood has resulted in a higher standard of illustrations than otherwise, and I remain eternally grateful to them and the many other walking companions, too numerous to mention, without whom this book would be as dry and uninteresting as many of my academic publications. Lastly, I wish to thank my wife Moira for her companionship on several walks, her support, and her tolerance of a husband conspicuous by his absence.

Preface

'Travel' wrote Francis Bacon nearly 400 years ago, 'is a part of education'. But it is also more than that. Many see the burgeoning travels of today's common man as a key to international understanding and world harmony. Others — more pessimistic yet perhaps more perceptive — see the scatter of the tourist dollar as enriching local economies while despoiling subtle cultures and eroding fragile environments, a typical Third World scenario yet recognizable even here in Europe. There is truth in both views. Travel is surely a two-edged sword.

Thus we who enjoy the wild places bear a heavy responsibility. It is up to us to do the right thing and to champion the cause of the wilderness. It is all too easy to kill the goose that lays the golden eggs. A case in point was the closure of the Nanda Devi Sanctuary by the Indian Government in 1983, jeopardized by excessive use and environmental pollution. Here in Britain there are comparable if smaller scale problems, although frequently it is already too late!

'Leave nothing but footprints, take nothing but photographs' is a usually well observed North American dictum — but no less applicable in Britain where the title National Park embraces an older, more mature and already well-developed landscape. Indeed, having witnessed the honey-pot effect of National Parks in England and Wales, conservationists have long stood out against the establishment of such parks in Scotland. The Scottish Highlands (Western Europe's largest wilderness area and the subject of this book) are desperately vulnerable, as the recently attempted rape of Lurcher's Gully in the Cairngorms has demonstrated yet again.

Yet native Highlanders must live and work,

and surely some careful development is appropriate in the *right* places? Perhaps there is something to be said for the establishment of a single Highlands-wide conservation authority with real power rather than several individual National Parks?

This book is one of our series of Long Distance Walks titles which sets out to encourage the traveller to undertake and enjoy journeys on foot through many of the world's wild places. Typically the series covers mountains or upland country because that is where the most interesting routes are found, with difficulties and commitments to suit most tastes. It does so always mindful of the points discussed above.

Most travel books fall into one of two categories. Some are guidebooks pure and simple, usually useful and at best even interesting, if hardly a 'good read'. Others are narrative accounts, readable, fascinating, often extremely entertaining, but typically ignoring disdainfully any desire of readers to repeat the journey themselves. Hopefully our series embraces something of both, entertaining and enthusing, while helping the traveller with first-hand practical advice and crucial information.

Arthur Stewart, the author of this volume, is a Physical Education lecturer at Edinburgh University and a graduate of the celebrated Outdoor Pursuits Programme in the Faculty of Physical Education at Canada's Calgary University. He has much experience among the world's greater ranges. In this book he laces a wide knowledge of his native Highlands with observations on mountain safety, survival and weather; crucial elements all in the year-round enjoyment of the beautiful Scottish hills.

John Cleare

Introduction

While Scotland seems very small for its population of 5 million, there are still places that can be sought, thankfully, where it is possible to enjoy real wilderness and solitude. As long as there remain such places, where the difficulty of access allows only those sufficiently committed to enjoy the riches; where individuals must experience the triumph or disaster of their decisions; and where the weather may equally transform such excursions into rapture or misery, the possibilities for adventure know few limits.

It is my belief that one of the benefits of such walks is taking the individual far away from civilization. As a result I have deliberately avoided making the walks longer than they are to prevent routes either following roads excessively (I accept that retrieving a vehicle may make this a necessity) or arriving at settlement of some form. I have confined my routes to the Highlands of Scotland, where I believe the scenery is the finest, and where the population is most sparse. At the risk of criticism for omitting the many exploratory possibilities of the Uplands, Lowlands or islands (where technical difficulty frequently exceeds that on the mainland) I make no apology for my own selection of routes, the painful choice of which has left out many all-time favourites. In trying to maintain a balance of short and long, easy and difficult, summer and winter, I have invariably excluded many areas which merit extensive exploration.

In this volume, I hope to convey something of the force that has propelled me for the last quarter of a century, to seek, to explore and to discover.

The Grey Man of Ben MacDui (Cairngorms)

The largest area of high ground in Britain has many attractions. The Cairngorm plateau is built on a granite basement and it houses what are by British standards giant mountain peaks; it features spectacular corries, and has been dissected by numerous rivers which flow north, south, east and west through ancient Caledonian pine forest. The high Cairngorm tops represent a special challenge to the mountaineer. Eight summits and four distinct mountains which exceed 4,000ft (1,245m) render the area by far the highest upland region in Britain and a Mecca for those who enjoy mountain sports. Having scaled Cairngorm at the age of four as my first 'real hill', I have always felt a great attraction to the range.

As the automatic weather station on the summit of Cairngorm will indicate, the area is as exposed as any in Britain in terms of fierce and unpredictable weather conditions. The high mountain bothies are no longer there, removed in order to discourage individuals from setting out for them under impossible weather conditions – a policy adopted after numerous ill-fated excursions ended in tragedy. However, treated with the respect that they deserve, the Cairngorms are a hungry adventurer's feast. The sheer size of the range allows enormous scope for the mountain walker or the valley hiker. The route described is a four-day trip which encompasses both.

October is always a memorable month in the Scottish Highlands. Firstly, the colours are on the turn and they offer a spectacular display of nature's rainbow, particularly when illuminated by the horizontal rays of yellow light at both ends of the day. Secondly, the weather may follow equally midsummer or midwinter patterns (though it is always best to be clad for the latter). Thirdly, the shooting season is usually in full swing. While the law allows shooting for eight months of the year, grouse shooting and deer stalking remain the major money-spinners for most estates, and their land is jealously guarded during these seasons. Beginning on 1 July, the stag shooting season continues until 20 October, and while grouse shooting is from 12 August until 10 December, most grouse shooting is done before the end of October. The walker disturbing a party of shooters or stalkers (who pay very large sums of money for their pleasure) is liable to be subjected to attack – verbal or otherwise.

And so it was that I set off in October with two companions, hoping to show them something of Scotland's roof and my own 'stomping ground'. Tim was from Cairns in Queensland, Australia, heart of Barrier Reef country. Mary Francis, or 'MF' for short, was from Calgary in Alberta, Canada. The three of us had all studied together in Calgary and on the

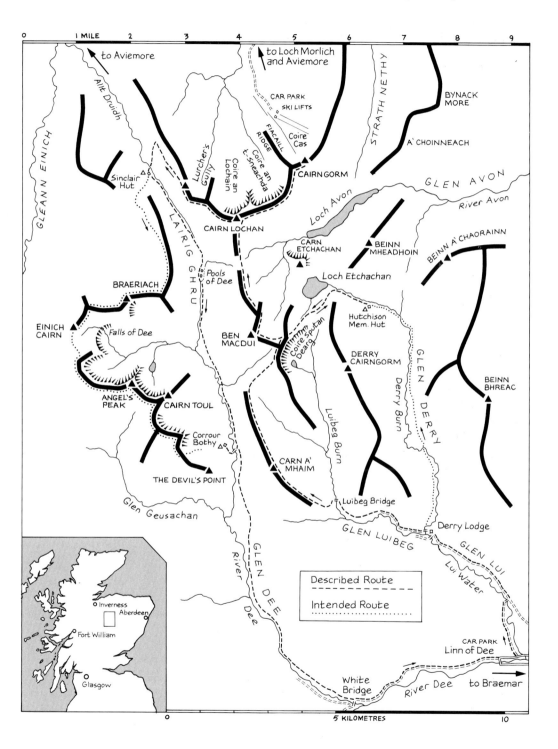

completion of our course, had remained the very best of friends. I had explained to them that it was shooting season and that the privately owned mountains were liable to be pocked with gun-toting groups who were driven around in jeeps. With a passionate distaste for blood sports and understandable frustration at the lack of access, we set off under a grey, late-afternoon sky.

Leaving the A93 Aberdeen to Perth route at Braemar, we drove the 6 miles (10km) to the Linn of Dee and left the car at the car-park a little beyond the bridge (063897). We relaxed into an easy walk up the track to Derry Lodge, the heavy packs triggering the mental inventory of what could have been left behind. As an introduction to the Cairngorms, the route is one of the most beautiful. The old gnarled pines that have withstood 150 winters line the river valley in places, reminding walkers that they are entering the remains of a forest that, after the retreat of the last ice-age, covered much of the country. The luxurious flat spread of river flood-plain was without its usual population of red deer, perhaps because it was the rutting season, or the fact that they knew the shooting season had started and had an instinctive fear. The rounded hills of Carn a' Mhaim and Derry Cairngorm swung into view — a complete contrast to the sharper ridge and valley topography further west — reminding us that they too had been fashioned by the work of glacial action. I recounted the tale of losing the seat of my breeches to Derry Cairngorm ten years previously — after a non-stop glissade from summit to valley floor, it had worn through completely, revealing a label and a smile, while my companion was reduced to tears with the effort of his laughing.

At Derry Lodge, we were halted by a deerstalker-capped man brandishing two barrels and a grin.

'Where d'you think you're going?' he barked above the rumbling of a waiting Land Rover.

'Hutchison Hut, by Loch Etchachan' I responded.

'No you're nae!' came the retort, 'Cross that bridge an' you'll get your throats cut!'

'We're sticking to the paths of a National Nature Reserve, and you're asking us politely to reconsider our route choice. Am I right?' I said.

'Right.'

Ashamed to be Scots with such an onslaught in front of the others, I suggested we follow another route and try our best to forget the whole thing. In the National Parks systems in both Canada and Australia, where wild places are subject to protection from animal, vegetable and mineral exploitation, the hiker is able to roam relatively freely. Despite England and Wales having had National Parks since the 1950s, similar criteria applied for establishing parks north of the border would transform practically the entire Scottish Highlands into one big park! Despite the superficial attraction, this would be totally unworkable. It can be argued that the big sporting estates which cover most of the Highlands have, in one way, preserved the wilderness from other, far less acceptable forms of exploitation, though there are both good and bad owners. Nevertheless, if the estates are to exist and their local workers to remain in employment, harsh economics demand that shooting and stalking be exploited to the full.

Somewhat disillusioned, we walked on in the knowledge that we would climb to the summit of Carn a' Mhaim before we traversed into Loch Etchachan and the hut that was not far below. With only a fair-to-middling weather forecast, we tolerated the cold when it was dry, but when the first of a series of squalls hit us, the others wondered whether their warm layers were sufficient. After we crossed the Luibeg stream by the bridge, the slope in front of us reared up and we slowed our plod for the ascent. There was a bite to the wind that became more severe as we gained height. Yet as quickly as the squalls

Luibeg Burn

came, they were over. Chilly as we were, we were grateful that our rainproofs kept us dry. At the summit of the hill, we gazed down on the only true ridge of the Cairngorms and saw it taper into the massive bulk of Scotland's second peak, Ben MacDui. Our route ran along the ridge and up much of the flank of the bigger hill, before we could descend to Loch Etchachan and the hut. The unexpected extra distance had caught us by surprise and the haunch of MacDui seemed interminable. The extra height nudged our position below freezing level, as testified by the next squall which fell as sleet and then snow.

'Croist!' exclaimed Tim, 'If this is October, what the hell is winter like?'

Although we ended up less than half a mile from the summit of Ben MacDui, we felt it could wait until the following day and that above all else, we wanted to get sorted out at the hut while there was still light. Just as our tiredness was about to manifest itself in anger at the stalkers (who had forced us to walk around three sides of a square), the loch appeared in front of its craggy backdrop to the north. The highest loch of any significant size in Scotland, it boasts a canoe club whose dedicated, if a little eccentric members carry their canoes up to 920m for the most spectacular flat canoeing anywhere in Britain. We joined the path that led the few hundred metres from the loch to the Hutchison memorial hut. Looked after by a climbing club from Aberdeen, the hut is one of the better-maintained examples of the primitive mountain shelter. Its earth floor was surrounded by stone walls that had been recently whitewashed. There were a few shovels and paint tins which suggested that work was still to be completed, together with a tidy appearance that was most welcoming, if a little spartan. After supper, Tim's candle reflected its light around the walls that allowed us to plan our route well into the hours of darkness.

The hut was located in the heart of a rock climber's paradise. After decadence had delayed our departure in the morning, we scanned the crags for signs of life, but saw none as we slowly regained the height we had descended the previous evening. The path followed the stream feeding the loch to its source, with the spectacular cliffs of Coire Sputan Dearg only a few metres away — a hazard in winter, particularly in bad visibility. The massive haunch of the hill was gained at the usual slow pace and the virtually horizontal approach to the summit, across the plateau, was a pleasant contrast. Walkers seemed to appear from all directions and converge on the summit cairn with its direction indicator and outlying windbreak walls. The wind had changed to a more bitter note that reminded us that winter was only just around the corner. Ribbons of snow remained after the squalls of the previous day, though in October, the Cairngorms are about as free of snow as they ever get.

After a brief rest and a snack, we continued north across the plateau past the former location of the old Curran Bothy — the site of the ill-fated school party's tragedy in November 1971 when attempts to find it in appalling weather proved futile. Although driving snow and white-out had obliterated all features (including the hut) and made navigation impossible, the irony was that the autumn snowpack was too shallow to dig into for shelter. Several winters previously, I remembered wondering where the hut was, when it was pointed out that all that could be seen was the chimney shaft — the rest was submerged under several metres of snow.

We continued along to Cairn Lochan, wrapped in all our warm clothes, the cold preventing us from stopping for too long. Although it would mean returning the same way, we decided to walk over to the summit of Cairngorm. A rough path threaded its way between the boulders and the heather, not far from the drop-off. We were peering over the edge of the Fiacaill buttress, the nose of rock that separates Coire an t-Sneachda and Coire Cas, when up popped a red helmet with a black beard, not a dozen feet in front of us. The climber had just topped out of one of the more difficult routes on the cliff. His bare hands and woolly sweater made us feel all the colder.

At the familiar boulder-strewn summit of Cairngorm there were many day walkers cowering behind what limited shelter there was. No sooner had we arrived when, as if on cue, the automatic weather station popped its top, exposing its various antennae to the elements. The reactions of the various individuals close enough to hear the whine of its motors varied from total disregard to mild hysteria. While the device certainly appeared out of place, its presence is more than justified by its significant contribution to the accuracy of mountain weather forecasts.

Leaving the top, we followed the cliffs back west to Lurcher's Crag, reputedly named after a climber's dog which had raced up the gully and up to the edge of the cliff, coming perilously close to plummeting to its death. As I gazed down the length of Lurcher's Gully, I recalled the winter when I had skied down it through a foot of fresh powder snow.

Recently, the whole area was fraught with great controversy over a proposed ski development. While developers, tourist agencies and downhill skiers were for the development, the majority of cross-country skiers, walkers and conservationists were against it. If it had gone ahead, the development would have involved a new high-level road providing easy access to the northern corries of the Cairngorms, together with lines of pylons for ski-tows and chairlifts. For all the size of the Cairngorms, such a development would not have been great in terms of area, but fears over the precedent that would not have been set, had the development gone ahead, contributed to its ultimate rejection. While the downhill skiers are up in arms, my own opinion is that as long as snow cover is less than predictable in our fickle climate, varying widely from week to week and year to year, it seems more logical that the skier should seek out the snow, rather than presume it will fall where most convenient.

Our path met the one from the Queen's Forest, leading down into the Lairig Ghru, the north-south valley that bisects the range. The Sinclair hut, our destination, was atop a steep slope overlooking the stream. We filled all our water containers before climbing up the bank. Opening the door of the hut, our spirits sank. The place was a cross between a refugee camp and a rubbish tip. It was filthy and rubbish was littered everywhere, thanks to some selfish individuals who expected others to tidy up their mess. Everything we had come to the mountains to leave behind was right there in front of us — crowds, noise, smoke and rubbish. Just as I insisted we get the tent out (it is always wise to carry a tent in case the huts are full, though usually occupants are most accommodating), some of the others made room for us and we staked our claim. The group from Dundee seemed very friendly, and through our conversation I came to realize that a crowded bothy was part of the mountain experience for them. Secretly, I was ashamed of the appalling state of the place, having spent many enjoyable days staying in the huts in the National Parks of Canada and Australasia. However, when the rain began to fall on the tin roof, it quickly made the whole environment infinitely more tolerable and we survived the concerto of snoring to face the morning well rested.

Strategically placed as we were at the foot of Braeriach, our route to the Corrour Bothy (the next hut) was originally planned for one of the finest rounds in Scottish mountaineering - Braeriach, Einich Cairn, Angel's Peak and Cairn Toul — a grand slam in every sense of the word. It is here, in the western Cairngorms, that the plateau is scalloped into the finest of horseshoes where the attraction is surely the absence of the easy access which the other side of the Lairig Ghru boasts. But despite the very best of intentions, MF had an Achilles tendon that was angry and inflamed and it became patently clear that the only way for us to get to the Corrour hut was by following the Lairig.

Hiding my disappointment as well as I could, I calculated that the summit of Braeriach was to elude me for a fourth time. However, the Lairig, with its 830m pass was no cakewalk. The path climbed steadily in the shadow of Braeriach's northernmost spur, and though we were making good progress, MF was clearly in considerable discomfort. Having completed a lengthy mountaineering route with them both in Canada a year before, I had developed great respect for MF, whose stamina, skill and experience were all greater than my own.

An early lunch at the summit of the pass was spent with discussions over the position of the cairn. Perhaps it was an illusion in the fine mist that had descended, but it appeared that either the cairn didn't mark the top or the summit marked on the map didn't correspond with the ground features. There was a short stretch of flat ground separating the streams that cut down each side. The prolific boulder fields housed a tiny lochan, and a little farther down, the Pools of Dee — one of the official sources of the royal river. (The other is the Falls of Dee, where a tiny spring tumbles over the edge of the Braeriach plateau, and flows east for about two kilometres before joining the Lairig.)

The mist evaporated in the afternoon, allowing us the finest of views as we descended.

Of all the possible vantage points, the panorama offered by the Lairig Ghru of the western Cairngorms is the finest. It is an arcuate rock wall that curves from one coire to the next, terminating in the most spectacular of peaks. Corrour Bothy was visible from a considerable distance and the time passed slowly before we finally reached it. Straight away, MF went to immerse her swollen foot in some chilled royal water in the hope of some relief. Tim and I took one look at the inside of the hut and pitched the tent. There were obviously mice, rats or worse inhabiting the place judging by the prolific droppings, and the rubbish bags had holes chewed in them. But once the tent was up, we noticed the blackest of clouds scudding down the valley towards us and we decided to tidy up the hut so that we could at least cook inside it.

In the end, we did such a good job that we were still there well after nightfall and, with torrential rain outside, we decided to stay.

Later, going back to the tent to retrieve my pack, the fiercest rainstorm left me practically soaked over a distance of a dozen paces. The wind was getting stronger by the minute and the stretched fly of the tent began to flog like an old sail. The night was as black as pitch. No outline of sky was visible above the stone walls or roof. The wind surged and tugged at my clothes as I felt my way along, stumbling like a drunkard over the tussocks of grass. Falling over the guyline announced my arrival at the tent. My torch had switched itself on and the bulb was visible by the faintest red glow. I grabbed everything I found and began my blind stagger back to the hut, knowing that if I found myself

Sinclair Bothy.

16

footsteps in the snow. He was so frightened that he ran all the way down the mountain. A variation on the tale relates sightings of the Grey Man to the ghost of an old man who had perished one night on Ben MacDui, having got lost in a storm and having failed to find his way down. The ghost was said to knock on the door of the mountain huts so that it might gain shelter, especially in wild weather. The tale recounts that the old man made it down to a mountain bothy and knocked on the door, but his companions thought it was some trick of the wind and refused to open it. By the morning he had perished on the threshold. Whether or not the sightings are some illusion like the 'Brocken Spectre', where an individual sees his own shadow surrounded by a halo of light, cast on the mist itself, no doubt the tale will be perpetuated for many generations to come, in these and many other forms. But as we lay there in that cold, damp bothy in the heart of the Cairngorms in one of its notorious storms, the legend seemed credible enough to dispel our former nonchalance.

Looking down on the Lairig Ghru.

knee-deep in icy water, I had gone too far. The moaning of the wind in the total darkness had an eeriness to it that reminded me of the tale I had heard a dozen years before, of the Grey Man of Ben MacDui who haunted the area. I shivered. I have always been afraid of the dark, to say nothing of things that go bump in the night.

Spread out in our bags over the plastic groundsheet, I told the tale as the wind howled, the rain lashed down and the candle flickered. The story was of a giant spectre that haunted the mountain. It was reported by a University Professor by the name of Collie, a famous climber who was also a Fellow of the Royal Society. Alone at the summit, he had seen a giant shadow, and had heard the sound of

We could hear that the wind had changed direction because from time to time the sound of the river would be audible. Suddenly the door, held shut by a boulder, burst open followed by a furious blast of wind. I grabbed for my torch and practically shrieked with fright when it wouldn't work. Why the wind had chosen this of all moments to move a boulder too heavy for any of us to lift, I had no idea. Tim got up and closed the door, rolling the boulder back to wedge it firmly shut. The rational explanations that the mind clutches for in such situations were little comfort as we tried to snatch bouts of sleep.

Then it began. Scratching. I wasn't imagining it and, realizing that Tim was also awake, I confirmed with him what my ears told me. It was not the rodents. It was something big; something substantial. Perhaps we didn't admit it at the time, but I'm sure we all snuggled closer together in our fear. A fear of not being able to explain in rational terms an observation; a fear that could only be allayed by the light of day; a fear that the legend, in whatever form, might be founded on truth after all. This time none of us got up to have a look. We just lay there, cocooned in our bags in the dark, waiting for the light.

At about 6 o'clock I was answering an urgent call of nature, when in the half-light I discovered ten or more stags standing in the lee of the hut, rubbing the velvet of their antlers against the walls! The scratching sound was none other than the red deer making use of one of man's purpose-designed scratching points.

In the morning we found the tent had let in water, but it didn't matter because we were heading home anyway, assured of a dry night. The stags were gone, but the blood stains on the wall and some fragments of fur were there for us to see. We laughed at the irony of the three of us having been terrorized by some deer — perhaps they were getting their own back.

Choosing the White Bridge route rather than the Luibeg, we had some 13km (8 miles) of rough track to go before getting back to the car. Although MF was still in considerable pain, she coped with her heavy pack well, and a local estate Land Rover picked us up for the last few kilometres — a gesture of genuine kindness that made me realize that all landowners can't be bad

and that co-operation with one another is infinitely preferable to confrontation.

THE ROUTE

This four-day hut-to-hut tour is 52km (32 miles) long and involves 1,950m (6,400ft) of ascent. OS sheets 36 and 43 cover the area, but the 1:25000 Outdoor Leisure Sheet 3 'High Tops of the Cairngorms' provides greater detail. The intended route to Hutchison hut by going north up Glen Derry is preferable to our route over Carn a' Mhaim. However, in the shooting season, gamekeepers are within their rights to redirect walkers, and caution must be observed.

The return route via the Lairig Ghru could be replaced by our intended traverse of the high peaks of the western Cairngorms. This area is exceptionally beautiful, though very committing once the walker has gained the plateau. Summer or winter, the route is a good-weather one only, and is particularly hazardous in winter when large cornices guard the edge of the cliffs.

A prettier return to the Linn of Dee could be experienced by taking the left fork of the paths that leave Corrour Bothy, which leads into the attractive valley of the Luibeg. Trekkers going up Glen Derry directly to the Hutchison hut will miss this particularly scenic stretch.

Skywalking the South Cluanie Ridge (Glen Sheil)

On every Canadian $20 bill is a picture of the famed 'Valley of the Ten Peaks' in the Rockies. They combine outstanding grandeur with close proximity, as if by some freak geological occur-

rence. While the Scottish equivalent — the South Cluanie Ridge is neither as lofty nor as technically demanding, it has the same aura about it that captures the imagination of the

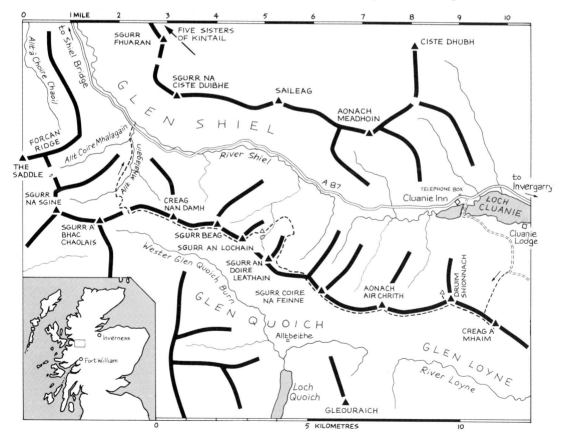

adventurous. The temptation for a traverse is almost irresistible.

Although not excessively long, the South Cluanie Ridge can be very demanding, even in midsummer. Where easier routes are also the domain of the nordic skier in winter, the South Cluanie Ridge is clearly the domain of the mountaineer.

Paralleling the five sisters of Kintail on the road to Skye, the route has imposing grandeur, comparable to the very finest anywhere in Scotland. Yet once the height is gained, the trekker may walk for 14km (8½ miles) along the ridge, losing little altitude between the summits. Whether the intention is to complete the ridge in a single day, or — as described here — in three, it is this unique combination of characteristics that has made this route appeal to me, and that has made it be remembered as an all-time favourite.

Driving west from Invergarry along the A 87, I stopped the minibus when the expected view of the so-called 'Loch of Scotland' appeared, with the South Cluanie ridge, our destination that night, forming the backdrop. From this point, the perspective makes Loch Garry resemble the shape of the whole country. It is well worth a look, and the group insisted on a team photograph before we continued to the starting point.

Turning left off the A87 just east of the phone box beside the Cluanie Inn, I coerced the twin rear wheels of the Bedford to squeeze along the single track road, hoping we wouldn't meet anything coming the other way. Following this narrow road across the bridge at the end of the loch and back eastwards for a short way, I unloaded the group and turned the bus at the road entrance to Cluanie Lodge, before finding a suitable spot to leave it without blocking a passing place.

We duly set off, and the twenty-minute walk further along the road was leisurely enough in the warmth of a mid-May afternoon. It served as an apt precursor to the exercise to come, loosening stiff joints and restoring the circulation to muscles dormant from three hours in the bus. The most logical point to begin the climb is the right-angled bend in the road as it crosses over a bridge (093094), although had we continued another 3km, a rough path would have taken us up the spur that marks the ridge's eastern end.

Fortunately, the weather had been comparatively dry for a while and the ground provided firm footing. The light grasses which can be such a fire risk were in abundance, and we were grateful that there was still plenty of water in the stream. We were able to do the lion's share of the climbing before filling our containers. Water is the last thing we wanted to be burdened with at the start of a trip, when packs are already filled to bursting with food.

The group shed layers before the start of the climb, which I insisted was a very slow but steady 'methodical plod'. Ironically, I believe this to be the fastest way up, as rest-stops are kept to a minimum. The grasses crept by beneath the soles of our boots as we ascended, our bobbing heads craned forward against the weight of our packs. Before very long I turned round to check that everyone was OK. Despite the very best of intentions to keep everyone together, I found that they were peppered evenly over the hillside. Inevitably, individual variations in fitness, comfort and motivation mean that larger groups are easily spread out, particularly on steeper slopes. It was well worth the stop at the source of the stream to fill up all available water containers before we gained the ridge. This we did by means of the saddle that separates Creag a' Mhàim and Druim Shionnach. An 'interesting' ribbon of snow clung to the very lip of the northern side, the last remains of the line of cornices that had formed over the winter. The snow itself was quite safe and presented no obstacle. A month earlier we would

Heavy loads.

have had to chop through with ice-axes or take a different route.

Once on the ridge, we were suddenly exposed to the buffeting winds that are the hallmark of an approaching depression. Early arrivals donned foul-weather clothing as they awaited the slower individuals, still clad in T-shirts. Even with such clothing on, we quickly became cold. The clouds scudded by swiftly, and bad weather was already visible on the southern horizon. Leaving our packs where they were, we walked along to Creag a' Mhàim's summit, whose impressive pinnacle-shaped cairn boasted a large soleless boot. Later, once camp had been established, we mused over how its owner had made his retreat (if indeed he had made it at all!) Even as we turned to retrieve our packs, the bad weather seemed to boil closer. A growing sense of urgency manifested itself in our increasingly

rapid walk back to the packs. As we walked, the ranges of hills to the south became engulfed in blue-grey cloud, one by one. As we swung the weight on to shoulders already tired from the ascent, we wondered how far along the ridge we would get before the crescendo of wind and rain hit us.

Scanning the map for possible campsites revealed little in the mid-section of the ridge, which was steep and narrow. Descending off the ridge's mid-section in bad weather could be ruled out, which targeted the area before the narrow section began. Once we were back at the saddle and moving with all our gear, I had a better indication of our progress as a group, against that of the weather. A group invariably travels at the speed of the slowest, and no doubt a smaller group would have moved faster, but as it turned out, we would have camped in the same

Ascending up to the ridge.

place, whatever our speed. A prominent fault line, some 400m north-west of the summit of Druim Shionnach, provided flat ground at the 850m level. A fault zone had thrust up a line of crags that afforded us adequate shelter, and although there was no fresh running water to top up our canteens, the snow banks were only an arm's length away from the tents. Following about 100 metres of tricky descent scrambling among snow and scree, we were pitching our tents just as the first drops of rain started to fall. By the time the heavier downpour began, we were settled, fed and watered. A swirling mist soon shut out all views. The clicking sound of the ptarmigan, the moaning of the wind and the patter of rain sang us to sleep after our voices fell silent for the night.

It rained all night. Sagging nylon fly-sheets that nobody could be bothered to re-peg during the hours of darkness would doubtless have touched the inner tents and let in the water, had we not found such a sheltered spot. Unzipping the fly-sheet, I could barely make out the other tents, let alone the ridge!

This came as something of a surprise, considering that the forecast said an anticyclone was building. Luckily, the wind had abated and the morning was still. One of the others muttered that the orange glow of the inner tent led her to believe it was a beautiful day outside. Staying put, resting, eating, drinking coffee and making a close study of the map was our strategy for the morning. While we had neither the time or the food to wait a whole day 'under siege', there seemed little point in marching out into the rain until it was absolutely necessary.

The weather had not shown much sign of change, so a little before lunchtime we regained the ridge with the prospect of five hours' walking in the proverbial 'Scots mist', before arriving at our next intended camp spot. Had the wind been as strong as before, it might not have been wise to continue at all. But with our

spirits lifted by the prospect of at least making a move, we plodded onwards towards Aonach air Chrith in our full waterproofs. At 1,021m, it is the loftiest peak on the route. With our 10 metre visibility, we mistook its false summit for the main top and our celebrations were premature. Early in the day, it is often difficult to gauge speed, particularly when heavy loads or bad weather enforce an unnaturally slow pace.

The group had split into a fast five and a slow seven. The five had no trouble keeping up and, like me, got cold waiting for the others. The seven, by contrast, were too hot and were continually frustrated when they finally joined the waiting five only to find them donning packs and setting off immediately. My desire for cohesiveness in the entire group led to thoughts of getting the rope out and telling everyone to hold on to their knot, just like kindergarten! No such moving handrail proved necessary after a chat with everyone and a redistribution of some items of equipment.

With constant checks on the navigation as well as fitness differences, it took us all of ninety minutes to travel the 2.5km to the ridge's highest summit. The top section of Aonach air Chrith is fairly steep, but we only allowed ourselves a brief halt. When we came to leave, I could scarcely believe my compass which pointed out into thin air (or rather thick air!) I had the feeling of being a skipper whose mutinous crew had forced him to walk the plank. I descended a little and found a possible route, but this led north — in the wrong direction. Tentative clambering down in the other direction was treacherous over the wet rock, but the path duly appeared, probably only a stone's throw away. It is so easy to forget how difficult and time-consuming navigation can be under these conditions, when in fair weather the walker merrily scampers along an obvious route and the map appears only at lunchtime to put a name to the surrounding hills.

The ridge became more clearly defined and our progress improved, though it was still too slow for some of the group to keep warm. Getting the temperature right is important, because the last thing you want is to get warm insulation clothing wet from perspiration. The need for warmth must be balanced against the ability to generate heat, which is determined by the physical work done and ultimately by an individual's level of fitness. The cold people were the fit ones, who had grown accustomed to a high work capacity producing a large amount of heat that kept them warm.

The path seemed to descend more sharply than the contours led us to believe, but I attributed this to the distortion imposed by the mist. After a while, you get 'a feel' for your rate of progress, which helps to pin-point position and reduce the time for navigation stops. Reluctantly, the group submitted to my demands for cohesion and formed one big caterpillar from the two smaller ones.

By the time that we had reached Sgurr Coire na Feinne, after its false top, the wind had come up and the rain was heavier. Despite our 'breathable' waterproofs, with the effort of moving, our nylon cagoules condensed up and we became damp from within. With such a concentration of water vapour, it seems possible that the flow of moisture can be forced to reverse, and the wearer imbibes the mist. Whatever the cause, everyone had got damp to varying degrees inside their waterproofs. Thanks to sensible clothing materials underneath and an improving pace, this resulted in only minor discomfort.

Through some trick of the bad visibility, either by the loads we were carrying, or as a result of our decadent start, we were all beginning to tire. I found the concentration of the compass work sapping my energy, combined with the effort of continually slowing the quick and quickening the slow. As a result, nobody was disappointed by my decision to descend off

the ridge at the only feasible point in the next 5km – the summit of Sgurr an Doire Leathain. This decided, we wasted little time in our descent, and headed north along a subsidiary ridge. But this well-defined escape was terminated by some cliffs, which in the everthickening mist, I nearly plummeted right over! I knew our route lay to the north-west but there seemed to be no way past. The route north-east was easier, but it led us in the wrong direction. I decided to opt for the easier route in the wrong direction. We had to lose about 300m of height. Although I was only half expecting it, a couple of momentary clearances as we lost height allowed me a sufficient window in the cloud to confirm my suspicions that we were indeed on the north-eastern spur. We were at a suitable height to contour round to the northern spur, and continue around to the lochan (012105). Reaching the first of these objectives, we were rewarded with a complete clearance. Our spirits soared as we approached what must surely be one of the finest campsites in the whole of Scotland. Hoods down now that the rain had eased to a light drizzle, we galloped the last few hundred metres to survey the luxurious grass at the lochside for the choicest spots to pitch the tents.

As we established our camp, the curtain of cloud slowly lifted higher and higher up the rocky backdrop. The ridge was up there somewhere, but it was difficult to discern whether the lighter patches were snow or sky. I took the chance to have a good look while visibility remained, to investigate possible ways to regain the ridge the following morning.

With a steady improvement in the weather, our damp things dried easily enough, and in the evening, everyone strolled around the loch and discovered a resounding echo as their yells reverberated around the coire. Climbing up the grassy slope to the north, I could see what a perfectly sheltered spot it was – protected from winds from all directions, with a beautiful backdrop and a bubbling waterfall cascading

High level camp.

into the loch only a few paces from the tents. This was the feeling of the genuine high camp that day walkers will never have. It was as if we lost ourselves not only in the beauty and remoteness of the environs, but in the timelessness of the mountains that were aeons old. There was no indication, save ourselves, of which century it was.

In the morning we were rewarded by sunshine through the breaks in the cloud, with the occasional blue sky showing through in patches. It was almost an anticlimax to have to break such an ideal camp as the sun's increasing strength dispersed the last wisps of cloud.

In retrospect, regaining the ridge would have been easier for some of the group by reversing our descent of the previous day on the spur of Sgurr an Doire Leathain. However, for trekkers of bold disposition, our route from the lochan directly up the 300m to the summit of Sgurr an Lochain presented little in the way of problems. It avoided the extensive ribbons of snow that lined the banks of the stream that could have caused a misplaced boot to slip. Had we gone that way, we might have regretted leaving ice-axes in the van. However, our spur route became increasingly steep towards the top. Taking extra care, we all 'crested out' without undue difficulty, the only dodgy moment being when a rucksack began a descent as its owner took a layer off to cool down. Despite the trickier climax to the spur, the ascent from the camp was a relatively swift way to gain not only the ridge, but also our next peak. The final rocky horn to the spur was the summit cairn of Sgurr an Lochain itself.

Unfortunately, not long after we had made our ascent, the cloud began its descent, demanding more compass work. As the group had come to accept, the Scottish mountain weather can be fickle all the year round, and the anticipation of another full day of Scots mist brought an indifferent response. But as luck would have it, we descended beneath the cloud again before reaching Sgurr Beag. As the mist dispersed around us, it opened up the panorama of the five Sisters of Kintail — on this occasion, five sisters without heads. Once again we marvelled at the clicking into focus of the visual sense which occurs when the mist clears. It is as if we adapt to the blur of the mist, with the result that 'normal' vision is heightened afterwards. This pin-sharp visibility was to remain for the rest of the journey and everyone relaxed a little, being able to see all the way to Creag nan Damh, the final peak of our route.

The sun's rays slanted through the cloud above us and although there were the remains of an old march fence to follow, we kept compasses handy in case the weather turned on us. We were counting paces as well, because the path that would lead us down into Glen Shiel would be tricky to find if the curtain of cloud did come down again. But even after the easy walk over the flatter western end to the ridge beyond its last summit, the ridge had one more surprise left in store for us — a neatly corniced ice wall sitting squarely on the spine of the ridge. It was composed of old granular corn snow, discoloured with the wind-carried dust of a dozen winter storms. It would have been a delight for the climber equipped with two axes and front-point crampons, but something of a hazard for the backpacker with neither. The obstacle was easily by-passed by descending a few metres down the mountain's flanks. With this behind us, the only remaining challenge was the location of the sinuous path that wound down from the bealach (967113).

The path leads all the way to the road and is a much wiser choice of route than the rough hillside which is steep and awkward in places. Because we were approaching the end of what had seemed a long journey, we were all showing signs of tiredness.

The continuous effort of thigh muscles having to resist the packs' overwhelming desire to respond to gravity, left us all very weary. With a large weight pummelling our shoulders into submission, frequent stops were required. The numerous cairns may assist the walker in finding the path in the initial stages where it is less well defined. As it descends, it parallels the the Allt Mhalagain, a stream whose delicious Highland taste will evoke memories of what is the epitome of everything high and wild — the South Cluanie ridge.

THE ROUTE

A one-day summer ridge walk for the energetic, or a three-day route for the backpacker, this route is 22.5km (14 miles) long and involves 1,950m (6,400ft) of ascent. OS sheet 33 covers the area. Snow may linger into late spring, presenting some difficulty for those without ice-axe experience. The limited escape from the ridge, absence of water and potentially difficult navigation make this a very demanding undertaking in anything less than good weather.

Access by road is straightforward enough from the A87 which links the Kyle of Lochalsh with the Great Glen. Although the route may be done in either direction, I prefer walking it east to west because the initial brunt of the climb is less severe and is over more quickly. While the route is possible all year round, it represents a major technical challenge if snow is present in significant quantities. Early spring traverses will require ice-axes for cutting steps in the old corn snow which may still lie in patches until July. (In cold conditions, crampons should also be carried.)

On a cautionary note, it should be remembered that once on the ridge itself, there are relatively few easy routes off. Once on top, the walker is committed, for although the path to Glen Quoich runs parallel to the ridge along its length, it would be foolhardy to descend to it carrying a heavy pack under bad conditions. Similarly, the spurs and corries to the north have numerous crags and small cliffs which could render such an escape impossible. Navigation can be tricky in bad visibility, but is the key to a safe crossing. Thankfully, the OS sheet 33 second series is very accurate and is an essential. Its 'one inch to the mile' predecessor appeared to have some 'poetic licence' in places.

The more energetic walker, particularly if afforded the luxury of good weather, may choose to continue the route over Sgurr a' Bhac Chaolais, Sgurr na Sgine and The Saddle. This undertaking may require another high-level camp and the most logical place would be the tiny lochan on the bealach of The Saddle itself (944125). This, however, is a very exposed site and should only be considered if conditions are ideal. Otherwise, the combination of flat ground, water and a sheltered site may necessitate descending the Allt a' Coire Mhalàgain until a suitable spot is reached. Once the Saddle has been climbed, the descent down the Forcan Ridge is a spectacular, if strenuous way to finish the route. It leads to a bealach where the route choices include a direct descent to the same finishing point, as our route (971140), or alternatively, the more gentle way of the Allt a' Choire Chaoil which guides the walker north and leads directly to Shiel Bridge.

Accommodation is available at Shiel Bridge (camping and caravan site and hotel), at Ratagan Youth Hostel (about a mile along the south road of Loch Duich), and at Morvich campsite (3km to the north-east).

Training to Ski — A Winter Tour in Ben Alder Country

I singularly moved to love the lovely that is not beloved; Love winter. It is not death but plentitude of peace.

Coventry Patmore

There is a certain satisfaction to be gained from travelling by train in winter. While the romance of steam is long gone, there is still the warmth of the compartment and the cold of the air outside. Cloaked in white, the scenery slips by easily to the reassuring rhythm of the train's motion. A small town slides past the window before the train comes to a halt. A line of station lamps, whose customary haloes contrast with the darkness of the early-morning sky, throw intersecting cones of light on to the snowy platform, plunging it into a hue of pale apricot. Steam exudes from underneath the coaches and even the slamming of doors is hushed.

For all their convenience, cars are something of a liability in Scottish winter weather conditions, to say nothing of the Scottish roads. Drumochter Pass is usually one of the first roads to be closed by drifting snow and, in 1984, several hundred motorists stranded in the drifts were evacuated by train after getting stuck on this notorious stretch of the A9. Train travel also opens up other possibilities that would not be practical unless another party were to do the reverse trip, or a time-consuming vehicle shuttle were performed. One stretch of wild country, beautifully accessed by rail, is that stretching between Drumochter Pass and Rannoch Moor. As a tract of land it links the two areas of giant hills in Glen Nevis and the Cairngorms, provides a truly wild and remote setting for a

traverse in either direction, and houses some of the most prized mountains in Scotland, which are doubly valuable because of their remoteness and the fact that they are infrequently visited.

Dalwhinnie was the starting point for our four-day trek, although variations in routes could account for anything between two days and a week in the area. In summer, the flatter sections of the route could tempt the mountain biker to gain access to the area, and in winter it is ideal for cross-country skiing. Backpacking in winter is equally feasible for those not fluent in nordic skiing, though some gentle downhill sections may be a little less enjoyable.

Our skis slid over the granular snow, with the familiar squeak of our ski poles as they transmitted the force of the extending arm. That old familiar rhythm, if a little rusty, came flowing back. The sun's dazzlingly bright rays burned through the still air. One day such as this each winter is all that is needed to recompense for the scores of other days when it is blowing a gale.

It was one of those rare occasions when a winter high pressure system coincided with a free weekend. More usually, perfect conditions during the week have a way of transforming into horizontal sleet at weekends. There wasn't a cloud in the sky as we crossed the railway tracks

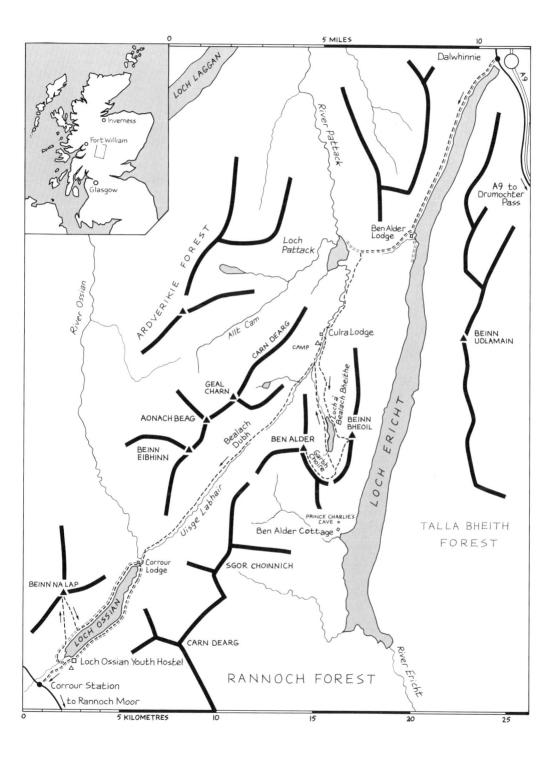

An early summer view of Ben Alder.

that had brought us to Dalwhinnie. After covering only a short distance, we realized that in such windless conditions, most of our layers of warm winter clothing would have to come off if we were to make any progress at all.

Whichever mode of transport is chosen, the introduction to this route is relatively forgiving. The first several miles are flat, along a Land Rover track that provides access to the estates further along the side of Loch Ericht. Our progress was measured by the ever-changing reflection on the perfect mirror of the loch which, apart from the occasional chunks of floating ice, showed an inverted panorama of the Drumochter hills.

The snow cover was not complete, and for once we were thankful for the strong winds, which frequently confound excursions to the area, but which had now conveniently drifted

the snow over the track. Much of the surrounding heathland remained bare. Shirts off, we slid along, with the occasional child-like chuckle as a manifestation of good fortune that couldn't be concealed. With various layers of clothing liberally adorning our packs, it appeared as if we were bound for the laundry rather than the heart of a remote mountain region.

The coniferous forest that flanks the leading edge of the scarp slope alongside Loch Ericht begins a little over a mile after crossing the railway and after a further four, we rested by the junction of the paths close to Ben Alder Lodge. The flat-topped Drumochter hills, where we had spent the previous two days practising our technique, were more distant now, but their deeply grooved stream valleys were etched by the slanting rays of the sun that enabled us to recognize exactly where we had been. The switch from light daypacks to full rucksacks seemed to accentuate any gentle rise in the track but I was satisfied that our skills had been well rehearsed on the steeper terrain, and the only mishap occurred when walking with skis strapped to the packs. This we christened the 'Van Gogh' effect, which involves one person bending down to tie a lace, forgetting the skis extending above, and coming close to slicing off the ear of an innocent third party. Afterwards we were all careful to give one another plenty of space.

Brief words exchanged with a local estate worker assured us that we were not the first to use skis to travel through.

'Right enough it fair looks like fun!' he had said, before driving off with his load of hay to scatter for the hungry deer.

Turning our backs on the loch, we made the gentle ascent between the patches of forest for just over a mile before arriving at a small rectangular metal hut that served as a shelter for all creatures great and small. The track curved away to the north, leading eventually to the shores of Loch Laggan, but our route followed a smaller path that led south-west to Culra Bothy. By this time the sun's impressive heat had opened up the occasional bare patch on the track, and from time to time a sickening whine of our ski bases grinding over stones or gravel would bring us to an abrupt halt. We were using waxless skis which have certain advantages over the waxable ones preferred by the purist skiers. The time saved by not having to prepare bases before you begin or clean them off after you finish each day, more than justified their lesser appeal. In addition, the more aromatic of ski waxes have a habit of penetrating everything in the pack, from clothing to food. A good friend who had been touring in Bavaria had an unfortunate incident involving a herniated tube of klister, the softest, stickiest wax of all. He told us that the group had left a fair coating on the glasses of a beerhouse in the town where their trip had ended some three days later!

The relative heat had produced a layer of water on top of the snow that provided extra lubrication and though we were able to move with less effort, balancing with our heavily laden packs became more difficult. The 'pull-the-rug-from-under-my-feet' trick was first performed by Paul who, with an expletive and skyward arc landed on his pack, a crampon point lodged firmly in his arm. As anyone who has gone ski touring with a heavy pack will confirm, the pack must come off in order to get up after a fall. This was the conclusion Paul reached somewhat reluctantly, our amusement at his fate making him more determined to prise himself up with pole-power. (Risking snapped poles in the middle of nowhere is not wise!)

We glided those last few miles to Culra beside the stream feeding Loch Pattack. The weather had held, and there before us Ben Alder and Ben Bheòil had slid into place like scenery on a giant stage. We were following one of the streams that drains these peaks, and could hear its rush beneath the snow. Though the cover was complete, we used the small footbridge a few hundred yards from the bothy. Murphy's law would doubtless have made one of us a water-diviner had we tried to cross the snow.

The hut, basic as it was, was inhabited by a group who were on Ben Alder that day, and they had staked their claim to the entire hut by leaving their gear scattered everywhere. Without hesitation, we unpacked the dome tent and pitched it nearby. We were fed, watered and snug in our bags by the time the four walkers returned, exhilarated but exhausted at their day.

'Those bastards have got skis, Kevin!' one of them said in a Glaswegian accent. He had seen our skis acting as storm guy stakes and no doubt thought that he was out of earshot.

A symphony of natural gurgles sang our contentment with our supper during the night, and with the battle of bladders well and truly lost, I lit the primus a little after 7 o'clock. Four healthy adults respiring for eleven hours in a nylon tent with several degrees of frost outside had produced a considerable amount of condensation. Saving weight by shoe-horning four into a three-man dome, we had to 'do the spoon' (all sleeping facing the same way at the same time) as it was. Those at the edges were the mops for the wet patches, though in our four-season synthetic bags, we remained warm enough.

Glowing with the central heating effect of porridge oats and sweet tea, I watched Bob pour the remaining undrunk tea into his water bottle.

'It quenches your thirst better than plain water', he said, 'and if you'd been roaming the hills for as long as I have, you'd pick up the odd tip like that!' Bob's teasing of a leader ten years his junior was good-natured.

Ben Alder, King of the range, lay four miles distant, and we were to ascend it, along with its smaller neighbour Beinn Bheòil, skiing as much of the route as possible. Leaving the tent, we negotiated the stream without difficulty and skied up to the lock on the Bealach Beithe, having to resort to a walk on the steeper section about half-way up. All the while, we contemplated the reverse journey after our ascent. It was a perfect gradient for an easy downhill run and the unique 'something for nothing' feeling that nordic skiing occasionally brings.

At the end of the frozen loch we made a depot of the skis on an 'island' that stuck out above the surrounding ice. Arranging the skis so that they stood vertically, but exposed only their edges to the wind, we thought they might remain upright and thus be more easily seen if

Camp at Culra.

visibility deteriorated later in the day. There seemed little point in continuing to the col between our two intended summits, for this would have meant a great deal of backtracking. However, no sooner were we committed to the unrelenting slopes of Beinn Bheòil, when the firm snow became frozen scree which proved to be both steep and awkward. Unlike the good soles of our narrow-heeled Italian boots, Paul's soles had insufficient grip on such terrain. As a result, he donned crampons and quickly overtook us before disappearing out of sight in the gathering mist. Without his advantage, Margaret, Bob and I shared the cutting of steps across the ice patches that were becoming more frequent.

As we crested the ridge an icy wall of cold air hit us, taking our breath away and the sun, which had been our companion until the bealach, disappeared behind a fine mist. And then a dozen shades of grey were in the sky — all cloud forms like teased cotton wool, all quickly moving. Loch Ericht itself seemed far, far below and disappeared beneath a stream of intermittent cloud. Our attention was diverted by the flash of a bosom-shaped hill to the east which was probably Beinn Udlamain. With the advancing mist, we concentrated on the immediate environs and the task in hand. The cliffs on the east side of the ridge were steep and heavily corniced, so we didn't approach too closely. Bypassing the large block-shaped subsidiary top, we found a less exposed way down to the col, where we lunched in the lee of a large boulder.

Ascending the steep scree of Beinn Bheòil was awkward, but at least the snow was shallow. By contrast, the way up Ben Alder involved the purgatory of ploughing through waist-deep snow. It was exhausting work, and as I measured our progress against that of the incoming 'pea-souper', I realized we had been beaten. As the visibility closed in — one hundred metres, fifty, thirty, ten — I knew that the only handrail for our navigation was a line of cornices too dangerous to approach. From that point onwards, when sky and ground had merged into the one uniform white, it was only the occasional ice-encrusted rock that broke the illusion of our dream-like state — a void in which it is so easy to lose not only a sense of cardinal direction, but also the sense of up and down. The classic dilemma faced us — to play safe and go back or be bold and go on in the hope of a clearance.

Even during the planning stage of our trip I remembered poring over the map, thinking the summit plateau of Ben Alder was no place to be in bad weather, but with so much invested in getting this far, it was easy to be tempted into believing that the weather would improve. We continued, navigating from point to point, ensuring there was terra firma beneath our boots, betrayed by the occasional rock. With exact pacing over the flat ground, we were confident of our distance and after 800 metres, we altered our bearing. This was another critical decision, for had we overestimated our distance, we would have been wandering about all day trying to find the top (as many people do!), and had we underestimated it, we would have walked over the cornices into thin air! However, some 360 paces after the change, the ground rose ahead of us, bearing the familiar square shape of an OS trig point, a great relief to us all.

We wasted little time with mutual congratulation at the summit in the hope of being able to retrace our footprints back to the col. However, the wind, propelling a layer of spindrift, had made short work of filling them in. Cursing our luck, we checked our compasses for the return trip, frustrated by our inability to move sufficiently fast to generate some warmth. However, the visibility slowly improved and by the time we reached the first haunch of the plateau the sky had cleared completely. We could see the whole panorama and immediately realized why the hill commanded such respect among hill-goers. Respectfully, we retreated, well satisfied with our judgement and our luck.

However, our day was far from over. Back at the col, we dearly wished we had stuck to our original intention of leaving the skis there, rather than at the other end of the frozen loch. They were just over a mile distant, but most of the way we were fighting through knee-deep snow. It was the combination of a subconscious relaxation once our goal had been accomplished, with the sheer effort of lifting our weary legs so high in order to make progress, that made us all very tired. No doubt the walkers at the bothy would have laughed to see 'the bastards with skis' toiling through the deep snow to where we had left them.

Our frustrations were quickly forgotten when we finally reached our cache, and after a drink and a rest, we proceeded to glide for the entire return distance remaining in one long schuss. It is this marvellous 'return-on-the-investment' feeling that holds the greatest attraction in skiing for me. The ease of travel by a self-propelled means, appropriate to the environment, promotes an underlying satisfaction (to say nothing of enhanced comfort) and makes greater distances possible for the same effort. And so we glided back to the hut, the occasional squeak of a double-pole plant breaking the musical whine of the skis sliding through the surface layers. We had accomplished the main objective of the trip, and had climbed our prize, Ben Alder, after coming so very close to turning back.

In the morning, the harsh, bitter conditions had been replaced by a humid warmth which had begun to thaw the snowpack. Scrunching up the condensation-saturated fly-sheet into the top of a pack, we hoped to be able to air it before using it that night. The idea was to ski up to the Bealach Dubh between Aonach Beag and Ben Alder and down the other side to Loch Ossian. This involved a significant climb and the traverse of an avalanche slope at the east side of the col. But if the change to skiing with full packs again was unwelcome, the alteration in the snowpack was positive purgatory. Skis adamantly refused to glide as great clumps of snow gathered under them. As if the unbalancing effect was not enough, when one clump eventually became dislodged, the ski shot away at a terrific speed, precipitating many a foul-tongued fall. It was exercise in its lowest form and frustrating in the extreme.

One at a time, we crossed the avalanche section, having dug a snow-pit to examine the pack's structure. It was safe to cross and presented no problems. At the col itself, the labour became less, but, if anything, the frustration grew! Waddling down the powder snow on the west side of the pass, often with one ski sticking like glue and the other gliding beautifully, our progress was laughable. Having recently joined BASI (British Association of Ski Instructors) as a nordic instructor, I was appalled at our progress and alarmed by the fact that our tracks didn't lie. At best, they showed a series of linked recoveries, and at worst, a succession of closely spaced craters, resembling a long message of morse code, written in the snow. My competence betrayed by the snow plastered all down my front, I was reminded of the long days I had spent in Canada, desperately trying to perfect the nordic discipline and return from each outing 'arsus intactus'.

After a long-overdue lunch, we were delighted when the views down to Loch Ossian cleared. It really was the jewel we had all heard it described as, a truly beautiful setting, the nearest public road a day's walk away in any direction. Our progress down to the loch became progressively more enjoyable as the gradient lessened, and falls became the exception rather than the rule. At the lochside we met Tom, the warden of the Youth Hostel, whom Bob recognized from a previous visit. He asked us back for tea, saying that the hostel

Skiing on a frozen river.

wasn't opening until the following day, but that he had lit the stove and the place was as warm as toast. The ski along the lochside was all the more enjoyable as a result. The incentive offered by such luxuries as a real seat and a cup of tea spurred us into a swift, fluid rhythm and we quickly forgot our previous tiredness and frustration.

Tom, having completed his daily routine of a run around the loch, joined us just after we arrived and soon we were drinking the fourth pot, happily exchanging stories as the sky outside grew darker. Tom invited us to stay as his guests, rather than sending us out to look for somewhere to camp, and we politely accepted. Unless the trekker wishes to camp high up, near the col, it is best to avoid the lochside areas which are regularly patrolled by estate staff. The

Youth Hostel is quite the prettiest in which I've ever stayed. It was once the ferry terminus for the parties that used to come in by train and stay at the lodge at the east end of the loch for fishing or stalking. The ferry has long gone, but the little jetty and its buildings make a most beautiful site for the hostel, encircled by old pine trees. Alternative accommodation is now offered by the bunkhouse that used to be part of the station buildings at Corrour, just over two kilometres to the west.

There had been a fair bit of snow during the night. The cloud was down and a strong westerly wind forced us to wear all of our weatherproof gear. The yellow light of the previous afternoon had been replaced by a steely blue, which accentuated the cold. The loch was a hue of gunmetal grey that belonged in Antarctica.

Along the shore of Loch Ossian.

We skied around the west end of Loch Ossian in order to ascend Beinn na Lap from a point directly opposite the hostel. It is one of those pudding-basin shaped hills that successfully conceals its summit until it has been reached. We left our skis by the track at the edge of the forest and continued up on foot. Without climbing skins on our skis, or release bindings for a safe descent, we decided that this was the only sensible way up for us. As it was, breaking trail was very hard indeed, as the powder snow had formed a crust of windslab, which every step broke through. Our well-honed navigation drill of sending one person out in front to use a sighting brought us to the summit, though the bitter cold and absence of shelter prompted us to descend immediately. Once below the cloud level again, we built a wall out of windslab

blocks and ate our lunch in the shelter it provided. Our boots, damp with the continuous scuffing they had received from the previous three days, seemed to wick water from snow to sock very effectively. After eating everything edible remaining in our packs, we continued down. Returning to the Youth Hostel by the east end of the loch and completing a circumnavigation, we were well over the hour which the warden took for his run. In fact, a register is kept of all hostel guests who complete the circumnavigation in under the hour. We were not tempted to try to qualify on our touring skis.

Cramming the remainder of our gear into the packs, we set off for Corrour station in the late afternoon. At the station half an hour later, it was ironic to see the notice threatening a fine for crossing the tracks, when the backdrop was the bleakest of vistas, without another living soul in sight. In the gathering gloom, the headlight probing the mist heralded the train.

As we trundled across Rannoch moor, several stags were visible by the trackside. The rain pattered against the window and we were content to be inside, in the warm again. Inquisitive looks from the Fort William passengers were returned with contented smiles that spoke of an inner happiness. Our traverse of one of Scotland's wildest stretches of country was complete.

THE ROUTE

This trek involves four days of walking or skiing. The terrain is demanding on Ben Alder and navigation is potentially difficult. Our route is 67km (42 miles) long, and involves 1,930m (6,300ft) of ascent. OS Sheets 42 and 41 cover the area.

In summer, or indeed for capable mountaineers in winter, the route from Culra to Loch Ossian could be made by the Aonach Beag ridge, with its four peaks, one of which, Geal Charn 1,132m (3,715ft), (470746) is guarded by an arete which is frequently snow covered until June. The route is demanding but spectacular, as it offers distant views of the Glen Nevis hills if you have a clear day.

Alternatively, the backpacker less interested in climbing to the summits may chose one of two further variations which are both very worth while. The more energetic of the two is to follow our route from Culra up to the col between Ben Alder and Beinn Bheòil (507703) and from there following the two parallel streams down to Prince Charlie's Cave and Benalder Cottage. Having had some difficulty in finding the cave from the map, it is not surprising that Bonnie Prince Charlie remained well hidden there. An easier route to the same place, but avoiding Culra altogether, is to follow the shores of Loch Ericht the entire way. At 30km, this is a long walk from Dalwhinnie, but perfectly possible for an adventurous group in the extended daylight of summer. The valley leading from Benalder cottage towards Aonach Beag has a good path, and excellent wild camping can be enjoyed close to the several large pools (458722) that mark the start of the path leading to Loch Ossian.

Star-Gazing in Glen Almond

The tract of land that lies to the south of Loch Tay offers spectacular views northward to some of Scotland's finest scenery. It is a stretch of country little travelled by backpackers and hillwalkers, largely because it lacks the higher mountains which abound in other areas of the Southern Highlands. However, this inadequacy can be seen as a positive attraction for the trekker who does not need such airy heights for pleasure, and for whom the prospect of not seeing another person all day long is itself ample reward. Because this area was developed for a mixture of traditional hill farming and shooting and fishing on the estates, the area is criss-

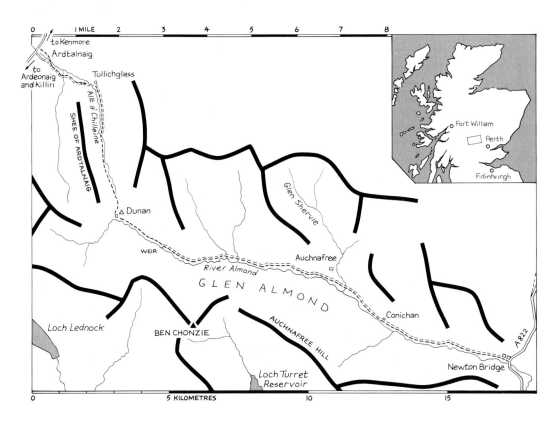

crossed with rough tracks which today are akin to what General Wade's roads were like two and a half centuries before — a rapid transit system for people through a wild environment. While Wade's objective in the 1720s and 30s was to build roads so that troops could be deployed quickly in the parts of the Highlands most needing them, the resulting military mobility contributed to Highland depopulation. His network of roads can still be followed for long distances today, though were they not marked on the map, their route would be less than obvious in places.

Glen Almond's tracks are well developed and this factor, along with the usual gentle gradients, allow the walker to cover larger distances more easily than in other parts of the country. But to infer that the area is in any way of lesser value than elsewhere for backpacking would be a crude misjudgement. The river Almond provides a most picturesque natural routeway across a range devoid of surfaced roads, down which cattle were driven in their hundreds as recently as the turn of the century. The ruined crofts and shielings are ample evidence of the population that once inhabited the area and provide a hint of mystique for the traveller who has an eye for the subtle rather than the spectacular.

Steve arrived with the car thirty-five minutes later than our arranged meeting time. His journey had been achieved at considerably less than walking pace owing to some 15cm of fresh snow. Most Edinburgh residents, no doubt having long forgotten the last time when it snowed heavily in the capital, were taken completely off their guard.

Both equally glad of a short break before the rush associated with the festive season, Steve and I had grabbed a couple of days off midweek to do over two days what in summer would be an easy day's walk. But with the daylight so short and the road conditions so unpredictable, we both agreed that a winter excursion to the area would be all the better for an overnight stop.

Long after we had returned to the safety and warmth of our homes, we discovered that a local farmer, aware that we hadn't returned to the car that night, had reported our absence to the police. Luckily, they were able to trace the car to someone who knew of our intentions and could allay fears that we might be in need of rescue.

The snow turned to slush and then freezing rain as we headed out of the city, passing lines of queueing commuters, city bound and blank faced. As we drove up the M90 towards Perth, it became apparent that Edinburgh's snow was highly localized, though roads everywhere were liable to be slippery. This pleased us, because we had left our skis at home — the frustration of having to walk through fine skiing terrain under perfect conditions would have been unbearable. As avid cross-country skiers, we realized that our first skiing of the season would have to wait. The joy of Glen Almond is its versatility for foot, cycle or ski, and though we had both cycled the route in the opposite direction, neither of us had skied it.

Taking the A85 from Perth to Crieff and the scenic A822 north towards Aberfeldy, we drove through the 'Sma' Glen' and parked in the lay-by beside Newton Bridge (890314). As we were sorting out gear into our packs, an ominous cracking sound came from the river. It had frozen right across, and the level had subsequently dropped, allowing the river-wide ice sheet to settle. It had been cold in Glen Almond for some time.

Following the public footpath sign across the bridge, we turned west and followed the valley, enshrouded in a heavy frost and a light dusting of snow. The rather peculiar weather system Britain was suffering at the time seemed to have its boundary right above us. A series of fronts associated with a low-pressure system straddled northern England and pushing steadily north,

Glen Almond.

meant cloud, wind and rain to the south. The high-pressure air mass that Scotland had enjoyed for three weeks, with cold, clear and dry, though frosty days, had prevented the fronts from progressing any further north. Above us, the sky showed cirrus cloud, which later developed into a spectacular mackerel sky.

The slight easterly wind knifed through our insulation layers once we had stopped. Whichever weather system we were in, it was very cold – cold enough to freeze up Steve's camera when we stopped to photograph ice formations in the river, and cold enough to feel the heat drain right out of us through the soles of our boots, a sensation that ensured that any such stops were brief.

We watched four deer hurdle a fence and continue an ascending traverse up the slopes of the hill. Their fluid movements had a natural efficiency as they covered the icy ground, but

the vapour from their breath suggested that they too were cold. Further along the valley, at Conichan, a farmer was bringing the last of his sheep off the hill with three working collies. Surprised by the sight of us, they bounded over, barking their playful welcome, yet immediately withdrew at the farmer's whistle.

Just beyond the farm a cairn commemorated the First World War victims who were residents of Glen Almond. It was built on the site of an old chapel, which gave some indication of the threshold population in centuries past. Today there are probably less than a dozen individuals inhabiting the entire valley.

The line of sun on the hill to our right became tantalizingly close, and at Auchnafree, bathed us in its relative warmth for all of two minutes. Without any direct sunshine throughout most of the winter, most of the farms would be cheerless places to work, no matter how

Afternoon light in Glen Almond.

beautiful the location. The sparkle of the sun was a just reward, albeit a momentary one, for our long hours in the shade. The high humidity close to the river had created long feathery crystals that shone like chandeliers.

The track wound into some hummocky terrain and once again the sun disappeared, thrusting us into shadow. These glacial remnants accentuated the subtle colours of the grasses and ferns that poked through the snow, like a pastel painting. The immense forces that sculptured the land led me to wonder how our route would have appeared during the Pleistocene epoch, when the hummocks were in the making. We would probably have been walking many hundred feet higher, over a heavily crevassed glacier.

As we traversed under the great haunch of Ben Chonzie, we observed the river icing up more and more. Out of the sun, we wondered whether we would be able to find running water at our intended camp at Dunan Bothy (740341). After the weir, the track ceased and became a meandering footpath with many solid ice patches to avoid. We plodded on, satisfied that we had sufficient time left to make camp in the daylight. Looking back, the summit of Ben Chonzie was starting to turn pink in the afternoon sun. Travelling beneath its steep flanks we'd been unable to see its higher slopes before, but now it dominated Dunan with a powerful aura of majesty.

One look inside the bothy told us that we would be using the tent. Its yawning gaps for doors and windows bade an unconditional welcome to all kinds of creatures. Though I had heard that the loft provided a good sleeping bench, much of this was rotten too and there was no ladder up to it. The missing slates, while no doubt convenient for star-gazing, did little for the insulation or shelter.

The easterly wind was stronger than before. Steve and I both thought that the sheep-fold would provide at least some shelter and be a sensible site for the tent (a special lightweight one which we had borrowed for the trip). However, the ground was so hard that forcing pegs through Scotland's answer to permafrost was frustratingly slow work. We tortured and battered the pegs into submission with the help of large stones, lamenting the fact that we hadn't brought my self-standing winter tent instead. Having managed to erect the thing in what appeared to be the most likely configuration, we observed that all it was good for was lying down in. Sitting and cooking was out of the question, given the agility required simply to get inside. The flapping of the fly-sheet was almost certainly not a design feature, though the draught responsible could foreseeably reduce condensation on a night as chilly as this. Cold fingered, perplexed and somewhat frustrated, we thought 'If only the tent could talk, it could tell us what we had done wrong or, better still, put itself up!'

We broke the ice and managed to fill every container with water. However, before we had returned the 50 metres or so to the tent, the water in each pan had frozen over! Not realizing what culinary joy lay in store, we retired to our sleeping bags at precisely 4 o'clock in the afternoon and proceeded to cook our evening meal. This had to be accomplished lying down, which was fine for a few minutes, but became sore on the back and on the elbows, which bore much of our weight on to the brick-hard ground.

Charged with the responsibility for stir-frying the vegetables, I felt a cramp coming in my hamstrings, thanks to my forced kneeling position akin to a rabbit's. I bobbed up, to be sprung back down by the roof of the inner tent, forcing me to up-end the pan! I painstakingly picked out green pepper, red pepper, onion and garlic sausage and discarded most of the grass and any dark objects bearing an uncanny resemblance to black olives (it was a sheep-fold after all!) I told Steve it wouldn't happen again. I felt sure he wouldn't taste the difference once it was all stirred into the macaroni and cheese.

By 5 o'clock we got ready to snooze, as, star-gazing apart, there was little else to do. I focused the binoculars on Venus, which only appears to the naked eye soon after the sun sets. Knowing that a three-quarter moon would soon be up and shining brightly, I explored the whole sky. It was still too bright to see much and, knowing it would be clear and cold, we huddled down for a few hours.

The moon appeared like a giant searchlight, bright enough to tell the time by, because of the reflection off the snow. It greatly reduced the clarity of the stars, though it was interesting in itself. The great crater of Copernicus, visible with the naked eye, seemed much more dramatic and three dimensional through the glasses. We retired to snooze again, in the hope that the moon would swing round behind the hills that had kept us in the shade during the day, so darkening the night sky. Two large mugs of tea each ensured that we wouldn't sleep right through until morning and miss the action. At midnight, I began cooking a dessert which warmed us up before a brief sojourn out into the cold. Once again our water had frozen up, rendering this a lengthy process, but shortly before 1 o'clock we emerged, filled with hot chocolate and pancakes, ready for more star observation.

The Big Dipper, commonly known as 'The Plough', has two pointer stars that direct the lay-observer to Polaris, the North Star. Because Polaris is situated in line with the earth's rotational axis, everything in the night sky appears to rotate around it, at least to any observer who has both sufficient warmth and sufficient patience. It also serves as the end of the 'handle' of the Little Dipper. Although I couldn't be sure without my reference chart, I thought I could identify the Andromeda galaxy which is known as M31 - the closest of the large galaxies to our own. Cassiopeia, Taurus and Cygnus were all visible, easily picked out from the faint Milky Way which was much more spectacular under magnification. The walls of the sheep-fold provided a firm arm-rest and made our observations virtually tremor free. But the highlight was undoubtedly Orion and, close by, the brightest of all (apart from the moon), Jupiter. Although its luminosity was effectively diluted by the proximity of the earth's largest satellite, Jupiter displayed three of its sixteen moons for us. Of these, four were observed by Galileo in 1610 with his primitive telescope, and one was reputedly observed by a Chinese in 364BC with the naked eye. But it was hard enough for us, even with the binoculars, given our inexperience and the fact that we were both starting to shiver. Steve retired cold while I waited to see a few more shooting stars before finally turning in for the remainder of the night.

Despite the walk not being particularly strenuous, we slept for a grand total of fourteen hours — more than two nights' worth in everyday terms. A tardy awakening left us in some doubt as to whether or not we had sufficient time to melt the necessary ice for our planned breakfast. With a carton of orange juice (mysteriously unfrozen) each, we chose to use the water for porridge rather than tea. After this, I was beginning to make French toast using the non-stick frying pan, when the old cramp returned and, once again, I upended the lot, this time into the tent. Hunger enforces a different threshold of hygiene and we salvaged as much as we could, mopping up the remainder with dry bread. With 0 out of 2 so far, Steve was glad that the only remaining meal was our sandwich lunch, which I had little chance of spilling for him, though I assured him I would make a concerted effort to do so.

The rising sun had noticeable heat in the chill of another clear and crisp morning. The earth beneath our boots felt as hard as iron, somehow accentuated by the clear air. We walked north along the track, through more hummocky till, anticipating the view that was about to appear ahead.

Meall Greigh was the first on the horizon. Capped with a sugar-like frosting of snow, it resembled Mount Fuji in Japan. It does not look as splendid from any other angle. As we neared the disused farm at Tullichglass, Meall Garbh was next to appear, higher, set further back and with greater snow cover. Then came An Stuc, the steepest and rockiest on the ridge, a black canine tooth pointing angrily skyward. And finally Ben Lawers appeared, higher than all the rest, like a great pyramid with one side mantled in blue shadow. It was a perfect panorama, with cloud lying below over the loch and azure skies

above. There could have been no finer reward for our journey in the shade and the chill of an early winter camp.

After an orgy of photography, we clumped down the path and descended into the shade and wispy cloud. We thought we could see ice on Loch Tay, but floes turned out to be ripples. There seemed to be odd movements of water on the loch, and rising clouds of vapour when the water met still, cold air. Nearing the shore, we could see the white rim of frost contrasting with the dark water.

Gill, our friend, had walked up the path to meet us. She had kindly agreed to drive us back to the car from the metropolis of Ardtalnaig, the tiny settlement marking the end of the footpath

Ben Lawers ridge.

Morning light at Tullichglass.

and our trek. Steve suggested that we have lunch in Aberfeldy on the way. 'Camp food just isn't the same', he said.

THE ROUTE

The trek involves 22km (13.5 miles) distance and 420m (1,400ft) of ascent. OS sheet 52 covers the entire walk. It is an ideal summer day walk or an overnight walk at any time of the year. Two groups could do a reciprocal trip and exchange keys in the middle to avoid the need for a vehicle shuttle. As a summer cycling route, it is spectacular and can be ridden in its entirety. Individuals doing this could always complete the remaining loop of road by bike as well, eliminating the need for a shuttle.

A variety of locations provide accommodation on the south shore of Loch Tay, ranging from Bed and Breakfast to the Ardeonaig Hotel. Individuals without private transport can take the post bus along the south road to Ardtalnaig and the start point (enquire at Killin or Kenmore post offices for timetable information).

An alternative route, longer by 5km, involving 400m of additional ascent and 7km of rough, trackless moorland, leaves Dunan Bothy and follows the River Almond south-west and then west to its source. Taking the southerly tributary at the fork (712333),.the route approaches close to the summit of Creag Uchdag at 879m which offers one of the best panoramas of the entire region. From there, it continues down in a westerly direction to the Finglen Burn path, which it follows down to Ardeonaig. This path is a Right of Way, though the stretch over the hill is not and may present access problems during the stalking season. The Ardtalnaig route is a right of way along its entire length and thus avoids such complication. While camping is not always encouraged and is not a 'right' as is access in this case, where bothies exist, it is common for walkers to camp nearby. As ever, prudent and tidy camp-craft will minimize any potential confrontations with land owners. Refer to *Heading for the Scottish Hills (see* Further Reading) for clarification on the access situation.

30 Miles to the Shelter Stone

There is no such thing as a river you have to cross.

Sir Edmund Hillary

Though travelling a circular route is always an attraction, a traverse from point A to point B has a commitment and inevitability that fosters a different excitement. A traverse of the highest upland region of Britain can be achieved in three to four days, with the return achieved by vehicle shuttle or, in this case, the Highland railway. With the closing of the car boot severing our reliance upon those things that support our 20th century life-styles, keys and valuables are zipped away into the less accessible corners of the pack. Map, cagoule, food and water remain close at hand symbolizing the shift to the real necessities of the present.

Clouds raced by overhead. Strong slanting sunlight illuminated the golden larches. Despite the strong wind, it was quite warm. Confused but content that the horrific weather forecast for the whole of Britain hadn't yet materialized, Steve, Moira and I set off on our three-day backpack trip, leaving Fenderbridge with its grand total of three houses. A brief shower of rain had us wearing cagoules right from the start, though we were grateful that for once the wind driving it was at our backs. All the way north up the A9 to Blair Atholl, the weather had been clear, but once we began walking, it had rapidly deteriorated into a more typical October welcome.

Passing by Kincraigie Farm, our route, a designated Scottish Right of Way, entered an ancient deciduous forest whose beech, birch, larch and oak all displayed different hues of gold in the morning light. A neat wooden sign bearing a number, the first of several we were to pass, indicated the route of the nature trail that began at the nearby town of Blair Atholl. We hadn't noticed them on our previous visit two winters previously, though they may have been buried under the fresh snow. The nordic skier, travelling perhaps twice as fast as the walker, may consequently be in danger of seeing less.

Our route gradually contoured around into the valley bottom, joining the riverside track, an alternative starting point, just after we left the forest. This, the twisting part of the glen (otherwise straight as an arrow) is especially picturesque. We had seen a large herd of about two hundred red deer on our winter visit, though on this occasion, their presence was betrayed by their calling. A cross between a cow, a sheep and a gurgle sound like unblocking a drain, the roar of the stag is quite distinctive. We speculated as to whether their harmonic bellows were heralding the close of the stag shooting season two days before, or were in celebration of the rut, now in full swing. Either way, the echo of one call had barely died away before another began.

By late morning we had reached Marble Bridge. The track crosses the Tilt here and continues all the way to its headwaters along the northern bank. From here the true geometry of the glen can fully be appreciated — as the map shows, it is as straight as any Scottish glen,

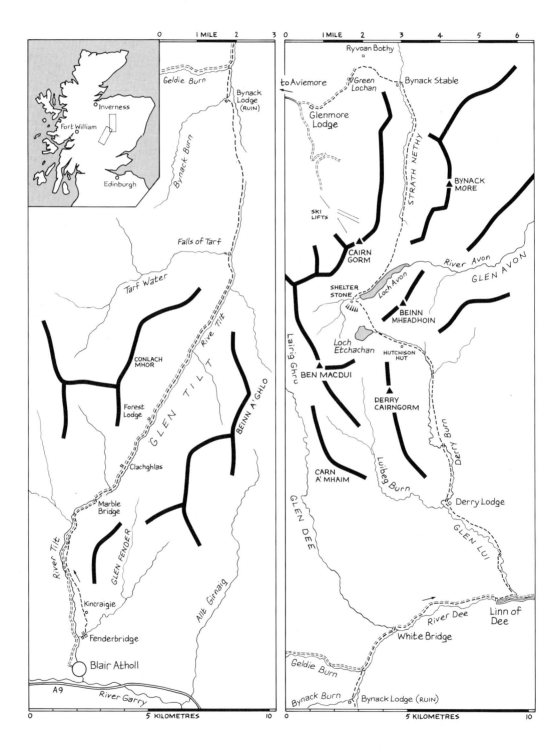

Birchwood near Braemar.

its symmetrical sides tapering into the distance. Having grown accustomed to the calling of deer by this time, our senses were suddenly awoken by a barking dog at Clachghlas. Menacingly, it bore down on us at full speed, snapping and snarling. While I normally have a bicycle pump for my defence when being pursued by a dog, on this occasion a sharp 'HOME!' ensured that neither blood was spilled nor goretex torn.

We approached Forest Lodge, the last bastion of civilization in the direction we were travelling before the Linn of Dee. Its singularly unimaginative architecture with plain grey walls is surrounded by a most picturesque forest garden, with over a dozen species of tree in autumn glory. The over-ripe rowans were scarlet, and the larches yellow against the backdrop of the hill to our left and the white

water of the rapids to our right. The side-streams that emptied their contents into the Tilt were white plumes against the brown hill. Their action had carved little notches into the slope, providing shelter for the occasional birch whose outlines collectively picked out that of the drainage. A particularly heavy squall of weather had us sheltering at the end of the larger wood to the north. The rapids were impressive in their creamy spate, and the eddies below were fizzing boils of cola.

Hoods up with the weather at our backs brought a strange satisfaction. It was exciting to be out in such weather without having to bear the full brunt of it. However, the tunnel vision created by our hoods shut out a lot of what there was to see along the way. We continued, the silence interrupted by the rain on our backs, the

Falls of Tarf.

rushing of the river and the occasional roar of a stag.

The track had been upgraded since the 1984 revision of the map, and continued wide enough for vehicles for another 3km, almost as far as the falls of Tarf. This is an impressive place, easily the highlight of our day, and obviously an overnight camp spot for those not intending to go quite as far as Bynack, our destination for the night. The falls themselves are cut into a rocky canyon which would clearly be impassable without a bridge. The Scottish Rights of Way Society, an organization geared to preserving access through traditional routes and drove roads in Scotland, provided a most ornate suspension bridge in 1886. It was dedicated to the memory of Francis Bedford who lost his life to the river in 1879, aged eighteen. Unlike so many other bridges, it has been well maintained and will no doubt last another 100 years.

Across the Tarf, the glen became wilder still. The deer were present in larger numbers and the verbalization of lust on the hoof was more prolific. The single path was badly drained in places and our progress slowed considerably in an attempt to keep our feet dry. The crest of the pass is ill-defined and the cairn marking it atop a knoll to the west, is not easily seen. Herd after herd of deer massed together as we passed by, several hundred metres away. Perhaps suspicious of our bright colours, or why we weren't sneaking up on them, they trotted off in their amusing fashion, the hue of their hides merging into that of the hill with almost perfect camouflage.

We passed Bynack Lodge, now a ruin, but once a thriving hunting lodge, which looked like an ideal campsite with its cloak of larches and flat grass. However, although we intended to cover a little more ground by dusk, our efforts were thwarted by inadvertently straying on to an island between two streams in spate (004860). With still dry feet, we were reluctant to cross so late in the day. We returned the half-mile or so to Bynack Lodge and pitched the tent in as much shelter as the ruined walls afforded. This retreat was really a blessing in disguise, as not five minutes after we were all inside, another squall hit with stormy gusts and torrential rain.

Fed, watered and dry, we listened to the rain 'stair-rodding' down as the wind buckled the tent poles. Momentarily, huge areas of the red fly-sheet pressed against the inner tent, despite the eight storm guys Steve had rigged. With the deer fallen silent, our sleep was disturbed all through the night by the intermittent battering of the rain during the squalls. Secretly, we all wondered what our river crossing would be like in the morning.

The rain had ceased, though the high winds and cool temperatures scythed through us as we left the relative warmth of the tent. One glance at the stream indicated that we would be wading it, a fact confirmed by a futile excursion a few hundred metres along the bank. Boots off, socks off, boots back on, we ploughed through as quickly as possible. At the far bank we coaxed some warmth back into our feet before applying our dry socks. As it was, they successfully mopped up much of the moisture out of the saturated leather before we halted at the bank of the Geldie, less than a mile further on. Somewhat bewildered at the sheer size of the river, particularly one that was unbridged, we realized that this crossing would be a much more serious undertaking altogether. I felt sure that the last time I had visited the area in the early 1970s, a cable bridge had existed, but that nobody had bothered using it because the ford, though wide, was very shallow. The remnants of a bridge of some form or another lay in ruins next to the hut on the north side, which was in a similar state of repair. On the south side, another river-bank foray brought us back to the ford, where vehicles could cross in lower water.

After the same drill as before, we waded in, surprised at how cold the Geldie was. Compared with the Bynack, it was deeper, swifter, colder and wider, and we wondered how we would fare. I could almost hear my calves groaning, contracting with the cold and its icy invasion that spread above our knees. Once in the flow, we developed a rhythm which took us across slowly, but steadily. The water that had flowed by so smoothly tugged at our legs as we teetered and shuffled our way into mid-stream. Steve braved going alone, while Moira and I hung on to each other, our boots slithering over the smooth rocks on the river bed causing us to make jerky movements in order to retain our balance. To any onlooker, we must have resembled well-lubricated drinking buddies stumbling home at dawn. The last section was the deepest and the swiftest, but seeing Steve safely across gave us sufficient confidence to reach the bank without mishap.

He produced the one luxury he was carrying — a towel! Several minutes of drying and rubbing coaxed a little warmth back into chilly extremities, though as soon as we started walking again, I felt my calves go quite stiff. Removing one soggy sock eased pressure on the Achilles tendon, though the looseness of the boot reduced my stability.

Passing the forest (010880), we realized how much planting must have taken place since the map revision, and we were very glad that we hadn't tried to camp in its shelter — we wouldn't have found sufficient flat ground for the tent! At the Dee (probably less full than the Geldie), we were very grateful of the White Bridge, the closest to the source of the Royal river. A lone equestrian was going the other way, and had we only met him a few minutes earlier, we could no doubt have been ferried across the water for the appropriate incentive. However, having covered as little as 4km by mid-morning, we felt that we had better get moving. We chose the easier (and slightly shorter) of the two possible routes to Derry Lodge, via the Linn of Dee.

The distinctive smell of pine got stronger as we approached the Linn. When we met day walkers without jackets coming the other way, we knew we must be getting close. Ironically, we passed a signpost warning that the Geldie and Bynack burns were unbridged and could easily be impassable in wet weather. We were later to learn that several people had lost their lives trying to get across in the 1940s and early 1950s, when all the huts and lodges (but not bridges) in the Geldie area were intact.

The Linn itself is a vertical slot in the bedrock through which the waters of the River Dee rush at great speed. More spectacular is the series of circular pools downstream, some approaching 10m deep, carved by the current and its load of stones. The black boils are treacherous, and given the steepness of the bank, it came as no surprise to us to see a life-belt strapped to the bridge. It was interesting to discover that in low water, scuba divers probe the pools, hauling themselves hand over hand along the bottom against the current. We understood why none was present at the time. Though the weather had cheered up considerably, we became cold as soon as we stopped. Ten minutes of lunch in the company of carloads of day-trippers, who had come as far up Royal Deeside as it was possible to come without resorting to self-propelled means, had us itching to get moving again.

We all felt tired in the early afternoon, and the 5km to Derry Lodge seemed like 10. Crossing the bridge over the Lui, we noticed that one large patch of mature timber had been clear cut, leaving a desolate entanglement of roots, stumps and dead branches. The deer, normally abundant in this section of the valley

in summer, were scant, though the occasional roar was audible. We crossed the footbridge over the Derry Burn and had a rest on a large log. Having come only a little more than half-way, we felt drained by a tiredness for no apparent reason. Perhaps it was the extra weight of wet feet!

The footpath, again provided by the Scottish Rights of Way Society, is far superior to the stony track on the eastern bank of the River. The soft ground and varied terrain brought the spring back into our steps. By the time we emerged at the bridge, a little more than a mile upstream, the calls of the deer had returned with redoubled frequency. The unmistakable three-peaked profile of Derry Cairngorm slowly revealed its flanks to us, with the dark Beinn Mheadhoin beyond. But there was an ominous increase in humidity that spoke of rain to come. We took the left fork for the route up to Loch Etchachan rather than the Lairig an Laoigh, in favour of an extra climb rather than the extra distance. Not long afterwards, the rain began, coinciding with the start of the steepest section of the path. A few residents of the Hutchison hut scurried inside, leaving us to face the weather alone. Sheets of rain, propelled by a blustery west wind slowed our pace as we donned rain jackets again. By the time we had reached the outflow of Loch Etchachan, it had moderated, though it was very cold and exposed. We put on all our remaining clothing and were duly reminded why the Cairngorms commanded such respect.

As we descended the steep path down to the Shelter Stone, the sense of remoteness was powerful. Loch Avon, the true heart of the range, stretched out before us, its steel blue surface pocked with whitecaps. Blue gave way to a green fringe, indicating the shallows, and a pink beach, ground out of the feldspar, the major mineral of the granite forming the bulk of the surrounding mountains. The head of the glen was an impressive rock wall, white water

Loch Avon.

Northern shore of Loch Avon.

gushing down the length of dark rock from top to bottom. Amongst the collection of massive boulders and debris, having tumbled down from the flanks of Scotland's second peak, is the 'Shelter Stone'. By chance, the massive rock had come to rest on two other huge boulders, forming a natural cave. The side-wall had been filled in by some sympathetic masonry, producing a very adequate year-round shelter for hill goers. However, descending through the blocky maze, we couldn't begin to imagine the massive event that had released such huge blocks, sending them crashing down.

Glad that we had daylight and good visibility to guide us to the stone, we still had a little trouble locating it. It is one of the largest chunks of rock amongst the debris, and the farthest west

of the really big ones. It has a cairn on top, though so do several others.

Pushing inside, I found it hard to believe that it was the same place that I'd visited eighteen years earlier, when an entire school party had crammed inside for a gloomy lunch. The saucer of light from my head torch revealed room for four or perhaps six people but no more. I was sure it had shrunk since I was at school. Looked after by volunteers of the RSPB (the Royal Society for the Protection of Birds), the place is made comfortable by a large quantity of dry heather flooring and a large plastic sheet for sleeping on. The log book, housed in a wooden box, made entertaining reading, despite some thoughtless individuals whose entries gave more information on drink consumed than mountain

Outside the shelter stone.

activity. We read of the mouse population, which, though silent for the present, was to make a spectacular appearance during the night.

The weather had worsened again, and we had reservations about how dry the place would remain in a strong westerly carrying rain. But once it began, the thought of going out to pitch the tent in the near darkness convinced us to stay put. Later we read of one group who had left the Shelter Stone because of the dampness to camp beside the stream, only to be awoken by water running right through the tent after the stream had burst its banks!

Heads uppermost on the slightly sloping bench for sleeping, meant a gale-force draught through the stone-built west wall, which successfully penetrated our sleeping bags. The occasional squeak and scurrying of a mouse meant rather less sleep for some than others. Mouse strategy involves waiting for the occupants to settle for the night before leaving their recesses and making forays for food scraps. One ran right over Moira's pillow, thankfully avoiding the opening of the sleeping bag. Gnawing sounds were confirmed in the morning when Steve found his foam sleeping pad perforated at one end and about an inch shorter!

At 8.30a.m. we awoke, having overslept. Content that we could average a sedate stroll and still make the 15:27 train from Aviemore, I began making pancakes while the others packed up. The mice were silent, no doubt still choking on the closed-cell foam of Steve's sleeping pad. The cold morning had our butane gas stove at the limits of its temperature range. Warming the cylinder with the hands significantly improved its performance.

On the move by 10 o'clock, we ambled along the shore path of the loch, amazed at how rocky and awkward it was. No wonder the mountain-bike fraternity have yet to penetrate the area – as one log entry related, pushing a bike is even slower than walking! The path forks a little east of half-way down the loch. We forked left,

enjoying the easy climb up to The Saddle in the morning sunshine. As the sun dried out much of the wet rock, the maroon became pink, dark became light, and the environment seemed less imposing. We looked down Strath Nethy at the way we had to go, knowing that it was all downhill from then on. In the distance, the ancient forest around Nethy Bridge was visible, though a vast expanse of rough heather and rock lay in between. The descent was gentle enough, though the nature of the path demanded our utmost concentration, so the scenery passed by largely unnoticed. There was only the occasional roar of a stag accompanied by the gentle bubbling of the stream. At Bynack Stable, we crossed the new footbridge and joined the main track that meets the Ryvoan Bothy path. As we wound in and down past An Lochan Uaine, the green lochan, strong sunlight slanted through the mixed forest, lending warmth to the early afternoon. A more picturesque end to a walk is hard to imagine. When the signs for the cross-country ski trails began to appear, we knew we weren't far from the roadhead and our destination – Glenmore Lodge, Scotland's national centre for mountain training. After a chat with a friend on the staff there, a lift saw us to the station in plenty of time to catch our train.

Rumbling down the tracks, the train covered in fifty minutes the ground we had covered in three days. However, it was a fitting reward to sit, relax and enjoy the view of Speyside decorated with the splash of an autumn rainbow.

THE ROUTE

This is a three- or four-day walk which, though long, has only one steep uphill section. After heavy rain, the rivers in Glen Tilt may become impassable. The Shelter Stone is a popular destination with groups and individuals intending to stay are advised to 'arrive early and avoid disappointment'. Our trek was 73km (45 miles) long, involving 1,020m (3,350ft) of ascent. OS sheets 43 and 36 cover the area.

The entire route could be completed equally well in the reverse direction. The reason we walked northwards was logistical, as well as meteorological. Alternative campsites are to be found at Derry Lodge and the falls of Tarf for the journey south. The slightly less energetic could spread the route over four days which affords more time to engage in other pursuits such as natural history, photography, or staying put for a day to dodge some bad weather!

To avoid the Linn of Dee, continue north from White Bridge upstream along the Dee, turning east before the slopes of Carn a' Mhaim. Follow the Luibeg down to Derry Lodge. This wilder, somewhat rougher route is less than a mile longer.

For those with an aversion to climbing, the Lairig an Laoigh path is much lower than our Etchachan route, though to reach the Shelter Stone, the walker has to cover an extra 3km on a rough path.

For those who particularly like forest walking, the track from Ryvoan Bothy itself, which leads the trekker all the way to the roadhead at Nethy Bridge (012194), is an equally beautiful finish to the walk.

Ben Lawers Walk — Alpine Flora and Ice-Age Flo

Were you ever out on Lawers alone, in the frozen sleet and snow?
The moaning sound you heard around was not the wind, t'was Flo.
For Flo was a maid of ancient times, who lived in a mammoth's hole,
Half up Beinn Ghlas, this hairy lass could eat a musk-ox whole.
In ice-age times, just as today, society had its classes,
And Flo's apartment on Beinn Ghlas raised her above the masses.
For Flo was proud, as women are, and oft was heard to say,
'My dear, I don't know how you live in the damp beside Loch Tay.'
But the ice-age passed, her cave grew damp, and the musk-ox fled the hill;
She felt the cold as she grew old, and lastly caught a chill.
A chill today, as you'll agree is quite a mild affliction,
But twenty thousand years ago, it usually meant extinction.
So ill and old, she staggered down for help from those below,
But they recalled her haughty airs and curtly bade her go.
She turned and started out again, in darkness, wind and sleet,
Such wind that night around Ben Lawers, she scarce could keep her feet.
Just where she died we do not know — some say Lochan nan Cat;
While others say she wanders still — the answer may be that.
So if you're out on Lawers alone, in frozen sleet and snow,
The moaning sound you hear around is not the wind — it's Flo.

Jim Cruickshank

Day walking or backpacking, summer or winter, the classic round of the Ben Lawers circuit must remain as one of Scotland's finest. The scenic rewards on a clear day span from the Cairngorms, Trossachs, Ochils to Etive (to north, south, east and west, respectively) and offer a particularly splendid panorama of the Highland battlements formed by the Glen Dochart, Orchy and Crianlarich hills. The Arctic/Alpine environment and unique geology has resulted in the proliferation of several species of hardy Alpine plants, found nowhere else in Britain. The treks described, covering opposite ends of the ridge, can be joined together to provide a continuous route (provided the walker is prepared to carry a full pack over all the ups and downs). The alternatives, among many possibilities in the area, are the separate excursions to both ends of the ridge which I have included here.

Since the establishment of the Scottish Ski Club hut in Coire Odhar (616401) which dates from the 1930s, and more particularly since the National Trust opened its visitor centre in the 1970s, the area has received high visitation. However, escaping the continuous flow of pedestrian traffic along the 'tourist route' up Ben Lawers, the adventurous can enjoy the freedom and solitude of those who, in generations before, recognized this particular area for its true worth.

'Were there really mammoths and musk-oxen right here?' asked one of the group.

'You mean you don't believe the legend?' I retorted.

The December darkness had brought with it a bitter chill. We were all huddled inside the

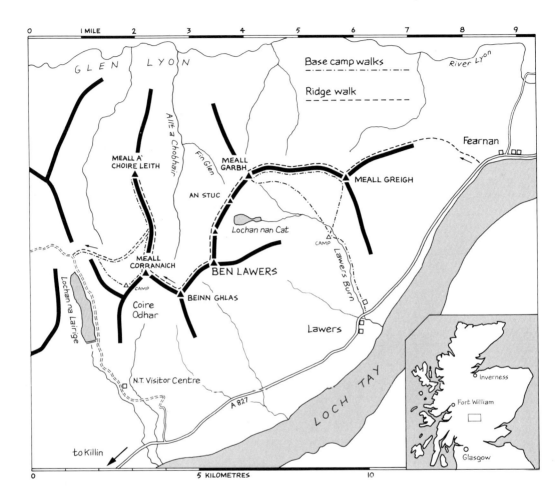

Dome tent for a brush-up on route choice. The course that had brought us together was a hillcraft class which I was teaching, where all the basics were introduced in the classroom and subsequently developed in the field. Having hired a van for the weekend, we had managed to tuck it into the car-park just up from the houses of Lawers village (680400). We had walked in carrying full packs past the Lawernacroy farm and had entered the National Trust land to the north. We didn't need to walk all the way to Lochan nan Cat to find a good campsite – the valley of the Lawers Burn made an excellent

spot well below the snow line that provided a suitable base to tackle the two hills at the eastern end of the ridge.

We were all gathered in a circle with the map in the middle. Three head torches dangled from the centre throwing roving cones of light over the maps we were studying. I had explained the details of route choice and navigation, and that it would be up to us all to put it into practice in the morning. I had indicated that the whole ridge comprised six peaks, five of which were Munros, hills over 914m (3,000ft) high which form a distinct summit. One individual considered Meall a' Choire Léith (612439) to be a part of the ridge as well, though I didn't agree. The discussion moved from navigation to the merits of hillwalking and Munro-bagging − the 'collecting' of all the Munro summits in Scotland. Munro-baggers have significantly increased the visitation to the hills, as evidenced by the large numbers of cars which appear at the base of most mountains with great regularity, every weekend of the year. The erosion in certain areas (including parts of the Ben Lawers path) has required extensive drainage and re-seeding programmes to be carried out, while the re-routed path directs the impact else-where.

I mentioned to the others that one day the previous summer I had completed the ridge in a single day, leading a group of army cadets undergoing officer training. Despite the difference in leadership styles with the officers, I had got on very well with 'the squaddies'.

'Tell us about the squaddies', I was asked, once we had finished the impromptu lesson, 'I mean, did they have rifles?'

'No, they didn't have rifles.'

The captain in charge of the cadets had wanted a special challenge for the group, which could be presented to them as a classic hillwalk, but that would be a test capable of separating the sheep from the goats.

'Come to think of it', I continued, 'they weren't even in uniform.'

I had parked the van not far from Lawers, the starting point of this excursion, and had taken the cadets up the grassy slope between the two oblique sectors of forest just west of Fearnan (712442).

'Did they have those black boots they wear on parade?'

I sensed a certain disrespect for the military among some of them.

'I don't remember − I was at the front most of the time, playing mother goose.'

A groan from the group.

'So they weren't fit then?' another asked.

'As fit as you lot, I suppose', I countered, 'but that's not saying a whole lot, is it?'

They continued to ask about the possibility of doing the whole ridge in a day.

'After Meall Greigh and Meall Garbh, our objectives for tomorrow', I said, 'there is an interesting nose-shaped hill, that is both rocky and steep. An Stuc, as it is called, gives great views down into Lochan nan Cat, and the remainder of the ridge, and may present some technical difficulty in winter.'

'Did the squaddies have any difficulty on it?'

'No, but that was summer. Drop the temperature by thirty degrees, add a little ice, snow, bad visibility, darkness − the usual par for the course in December − and you're operating under a totally different set of rules.'

'Was An Stuc a harder climb than Ben Lawers itself?'

'Not really − remember that was in summer. Ben Lawers is the biggest on the ridge by a considerable margin. By contrast, Ben Ghlas was easy for them. After the long steep descent from Lawers, the path up Ben Ghlas seemed almost flat.'

'Was that the last one?'

'No, but it was where it got very interesting for some of them. The drop down to the col between Ben Ghlas and Meall Corranaich is long and steep. Half of the group wanted to go down then.'

'But you didn't let them, did you?' they enthused.

'Well, no. Their Commanding Officer didn't let them.' Another groan from the group. They were enjoying this.

'Some of them had got blisters, and others had become a little dehydrated. But they all stuck it out till the end.'

'And where exactly was the end?'

'The end for the group was the Ben Lawers Visitor Centre − the one I have been telling you about.'

'And what about you?'

'Well, at the Centre, the Commanding Officer and I left our kit with the others, donned running shoes, and jogged back the 13 kilometres for the van.' A groan, louder than any of the others.

'So you see, it's perfectly possible to do the whole ridge in a day.'

In the morning, an amber light spilled down the narrow river valley, the line of shadows slowly descending the bank, until our camp was plunged into brilliant sunshine. There had been a good fall of snow during the night. Ice-axes and crampons were the order of the day, as the crisp conditions would no doubt have left a treacherous crust on the tops.

Meall Garbh.

After breakfast, we filed up the valley, crossing a series of streams that drained the hills to the south. Our strategy was to climb up to the col between the two hills (658440), ascend Meall Garbh first, and then Meall Greigh. I had various 'students' lead the way, keeping a check on the navigation as bad weather was approaching. Before we reached the col, the cloud had come right down and visibility was 20 metres or so. It was perfect for navigation practice. At the top, in the short time required for a team photograph, we were all bitterly chilled, despite being clad in all our winter gear. The wind — straight out of the north — was very strong, blasting exposed cheeks with ice. We formed a long line, enabling those without responsibility for navigating to 'tuck in' behind the person in front. This afforded some shelter and relative comfort for those without snow goggles.

Despite the cold having formed much windslab already, we had no difficulty in punching through the crust, and crampons were not needed. I let other members of the group do the navigation to Meall Greigh, glad that the cloud hadn't lifted, making it more of a challenge. As it was, the land, seen in circles only 20 metres across at a time, provided sufficient difficulty to render the lesson quite valuable. I had shown the group how to use each other, when there isn't anything else to sight onto with the compass, painfully slow and cold as it was. One student confessed to contouring around in a full circle on the only occasion he had encountered similar conditions before. Without a compass, such 'seat of the pants' navigation is often futile.

As we descended below 700m or so, the visibility improved and then cleared completely, allowing us to see a grand panorama of Loch Tay and the lower hills beyond. With the extra effort of punching through the snow, the party was quite content with the two peaks we had climbed, though I heard two of them

Lawers Burn valley and Loch Tay.

whisper to each other that they would return in midsummer and try to do the whole ridge in a day because 'if the squaddies could do it, we can do it'.

Later, the same winter, a different survival course explored the other end of the Lawers ridge.

'You'd better hope it's cold, laddie, or you'll not forget the night you spent in a snowhole for a long time.'

It had seemed so strange at the time, yet here was I, almost at the summit of Meall Corranaich, repeating virtually word for word the same advice that I had received as a student, more than a decade previously.

The climax of our winter mountaineering course, a night in a snow-hole, was potentially the most or least enjoyable part. According to the weather, the snowpack and the degree of luck, a night can be warm and snug, or cold, wet and thoroughly miserable. The colder the air temperature, the less likely any construction is to melt with the heat of respiring bodies and the greater the chance of spending a dry night. I remembered awaking amidst a pool of meltwater that had refrozen, like a swan frozen into the ice on a pond. My hair had frozen to the wall, none of the zips on any of my shell clothing would move and my boots were totally rigid in the morning. Experience, I had discovered, is the best teacher, provided you live through it.

'Now we're here, I'll just remind you of a few important things when building a snow shelter', I howled above the wind. 'The first thing is that you get very, very wet, and complete water-

61

proofs are essential.' Looking at the group, only half were wearing theirs, the others having shed layers during the slog up from the road to the 900m level where we were standing.

'The second thing is not to leave anything lying around — it will disappear beneath the snow you dig out. Every spring we find plates, cutlery, flasks, gloves, the occasional student, you name it, right here.' A ripple of laughter spread throughout the group. They were getting cold. I got them to start digging.

'And lastly', I said, 'nobody go upslope from the line of the cut, or else, just when it's getting dark and everyone else is inside their hole, we'll have to start again somewhere else.' The roof, given the depth of snow we had to work with, would be too thin to support a nocturnal wanderer.

Dennis Rewt, my friend and colleague, came over for a chat. While we both agreed that delegation was necessary to allow the students the benefit of the learning experience, the fact that we were to spend the night in the same shelters meant that we both did more than our fair share to ensure that the long hours of darkness would be passed as comfortably as possible. Dennis had already amused the groups with his antics, 'skiing' down atop his shovel. Now he suggested we demolish the wall between our shelters and make a cathedral. I agreed, but cautioned him about the year one group tried to do the same without telling us, razoring through the snow with saws, ice-axes and shovels while everyone was asleep. Neither of us wanted to make a student kebab by accident — it would be deliberate or not at all!

We admired each others' group shelter. They

Navigation work.

Winter survival — ice-axe work.

weren't great, but both were adequate for our purposes. The snow shelters we had built were suitable for a steep bank of snow and were a cross between an excavation and a construction. The blocks that were removed from the 'cave', were all used to cover over the entrance tunnel. It made a most efficient use of time and effort, provided of course, a suitable bank of snow was selected to begin with. Discovering grass with the shovel brought a string of unprintables which indicated a poor choice of snow bank, signalling the need to try elsewhere.

Dennis and I returned to our respective groups, in anticipation of our annual binge of sleep. With watches a little shy of 6 o'clock, we were all tucked up for the night.

The previous day the group had been practising ice-axe self-arrest on the various slopes on the west end of the Lawers ridge. We had begun at the Visitor Centre and continued up past the old ski hut (615401) and, rather than going up on to Beinn Ghlas by the 'tourist route' had gone through to the col between it and Corranaich. This way follows an old drove road that is still a good path. Cattle were driven from the farms in Glen Lyon across the pass and down to Lawers village, where they were taken by boat across to Ardtalnaig and finally to the market at Comrie, a natural confluence of early routeways. Snow nearly always collects to the north side of Coire Odhar, even when scant elsewhere.

We reached the col between Beinn Ghlas and Lawers itself after an exhilarating traverse across steep, though stable snow. Part of the course had included avalanche awareness, and during a brief rest, I dug a snow pit so the group could

Winter scrambling.

examine the different layers. It was consolidated, mostly corn snow, without any layers which could 'glide' over one another, which might have made it prone to avalanche.

The full force of the eastern wind hit us when we came out of the shelter of Beinn Ghlas. I explained that it was quite common for easterly winds to prevail during the winters, blowing straight across continental Europe from Siberia. The result is that the snow-loading on avalanche-prone slopes occurs in quite a different pattern from when westerly winds are blowing. Snow tends to accumulate in the lee of obstacles, so it follows that one wind will deposit snow in a gully while an opposite wind will scour it clean. I emphasized to the group that weather history forms a crucial part of avalanche awareness and avoidance.

The steep climb up to the summit of Ben Lawers required the use of ice-axes, more for stability in the high wind, than for the cutting of steps. As we inched our way up the pyramid of white that forms Scotland's ninth highest peak, it became easy for us to see how much more vulnerable and exposed a person becomes when the wind renders communication all but impossible. The flogging of our cagoules in our ears sounded like pistol shots. Because the summit itself has a steep drop-off to the north, I collected the entire group together on the flatter ground just below. The wind was so strong that one of our ice-axes almost blew away across the frozen ground. I took the group in pairs up to the summit, the three of us linking arms like Antarctic explorers.

'We're just going for a short walk', I yelled

Caledonian Pine forest near Derry Lodge.

Ascending the flanks of Ben MacDui (Carn a' Mhaim in the background).

Loch Etchachan.

'Loch of Scotland'.

*South Cluanie Ridge —
bad weather
approaching.*

*South Cluanie Ridge —
bad weather arrived.*

Loch Ericht, a mirror.

'Hot'. (Photo by Paul Jarvis.)

Loch Ericht, looking east.

Cattle in Glen Almond.

Morning light at Dunan.

The Lawers ridge in a temperature inversion.

Rowan colours.

Scottish Rights of Way Society's footbridge at the Tarf.

Loch Avon — western end.

The shelter stone.

Ben Lawers in summer — temperature inversion. (Photo by Dennis Rewt.)

Ice axe self-arrest practice.

Simon, at the summit of Mam Carraigh.

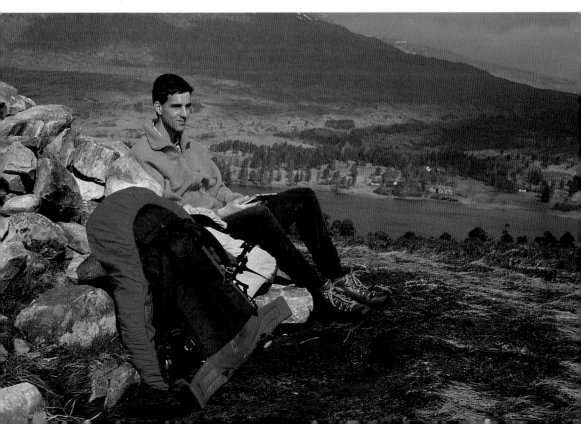

Approaching squall, Glen Kinglass.

Lochan nam Breac under evening light.

'Cresting out' at Màm Barrisdale.

The author.

Camp at Lochan nam Breac.

Ascending Ruadh-stac Mhór, Triple Buttress in the background.

Camp at Dubh-Lochain.

Deer at Barrisdale.

Bivouac site.

Early morning on the Beinn Eighe ridge.

Bog cotton near Blairmore.

Steve Senior, poised on the brink.

The cleft, Cape Wrath.

Lewisian Gneiss — contorted rock.

Sunset at Sandwood Bay.

as I departed with each pair, not knowing if their schooling had included Captain Oates' famous last words or not, 'we may be some time'.

By the time everyone had had their turn at the top, there was a unanimous decision to get moving again. The day hadn't been as clear as many previous visits, but the students were all impressed at the spectacular panorama Ben Lawers creates as a result of its extra height. They all agreed on the great character and beauty of the 'two-col' route up the mountain. It was more attractive, more exciting and less populated than the main route, though, as I warned them, it wasn't for following 'willy nilly' — it was important to gauge the snow stability if it was present in large quantities.

Emerging from a snow-hole bivouac.

Another danger, I had told them, was to think that the day was over when you got to the top of something. Reinforcing my point that more accidents happen on the way down, one of them slid, skidding for a dozen metres or so before his axe gained purchase through the crust. He was quite unhurt, though considerably less jubilant on the remainder of the descent.

The excitement of the previous day was overshadowed by the present-day task. Two stoves were purring in one corner, both melting panfuls of snow. One student was still outside, adding finishing touches to the roof; another was smoothing off the ceiling to avoid drips falling on us during the night; yet another was coercing some warmth into his toes, dismayed that his boots had let in water. When the other student arrived, he confirmed my suspicion that the wind was getting stronger.

'At least we won't have to worry about the tent blowing down!' I joked. My concern was only over the possibility of being drifted over during the night. It was paramount that we kept the entrance free to allow an adequate circulation of air. Because it was so peacefully quiet inside the shelter, it was all-too-tempting to believe it was peaceful outside as well. We had arranged several candles around the inside of the walls, to save our head-torch batteries.

'It was still dark and I was making the porridge.' I said, recounting the story of my first night in a snow-hole. 'In those days, a head-torch had wires all over the place, terminals that were covered in acid, and a battery the size of a half-brick that you wore round your waist. With all that rigmarole, it was no wonder that the things gave us trouble. Anyway, one of the leaders came over to have a look at it, and, applying some of his own blend of gentle persuasion, successfully propelled four and a half volts of Exide into the porridge!'

'You know', he had said, 'nine times out of ten, all you need is a little ingenuity to screw things up good and proper!'

A snow shelter makes an excellent bivouac.

'To this day, they never knew why their porridge tasted so funny.' We all laughed.

Settled down for the night, I had been wondering how the students would react to going out again, when one of the group surprised me by asking if we could climb to the top at night. It brought a mixed reception, but I suggested that we went up as a group or not at all.

The visibility had improved, making it perfectly possible to find our way without head-torches. The clear starry sky was more than enough to illuminate the white carpet of snow, and we were glad that the wind had dropped. It was 11.30 p.m. I forced everyone to go slowly, because in the half-light it was much harder to judge the slopes, and easier to lose your footing. The top brought mutual congratulation and a real sense of achievement.

'Being able to look after yourselves in winter on Scotland's mountains is something that we can't hope to teach in a week-long course. We can give you information and hone your skills, but we can't give you judgement. You have to develop that for yourselves over a number of years. But if we've given you the confidence to go to the hills, knowing the limits of your capabilities and having a healthy respect for the environment as you gain experience, at least we'll have achieved something.'

The ridge stretched away down to the col, with Beinn Ghlas and Ben Lawers behind. It was both inviting and magnificent, the crisp snow squeaking with our steps. A pale yellow moon was just nudging its way above the horizon to the east, sending a shaft of light reflecting over the silvery waters of Loch Tay.

'I'd like to climb the other hills on the ridge — the ones we saw yesterday from Lawers', said one of them.

'I'd like to do the whole ridge in a day!' said another, and, turning to me, 'D'you think we'll ever manage the whole ridge in a single day?'

'One day', I said, shrugging my shoulders with the chill of the night air, 'maybe'.

THE ROUTE

The Ben Lawers ridge walk represents a strenuous day walk in summer — 20km (12½ miles) long with 2,040m (6,700ft) of ascent. The base-camp approach for the two excursions cited may suit the backpacker who wishes to do more than cover the ground as quickly as possible.

Meall Garbh and Meall Greigh — 13km (8 miles), 1,070m (3,500ft) ascent; Meall Corranaich and Meall Coire a' Léith — 11km (7 miles), 720m (2,400ft) ascent. OS sheet 51 covers all of these routes. Much of the area is owned by the National Trust, which tolerates camping in certain locations. The area is world renowned for the Alpine plants which are unique to the area. Further information on these and all other aspects of the area's natural history is available from the Ben Lawers Visitor Centre which is open from spring to autumn.

The practice of snow-holing is potentially hazardous and should be undertaken only in the company of experienced companions. Comfortable snow shelters require suitable snow and equipment, and take skill, time and patience to build.

Glen Kinglass and the Anatomy of a Depression

I could remember it all so clearly as we huddled together in Tim's tent. Not by any stretch of the imagination could it be termed a three-man tent – even for the close friends that we were. Tim, Alice and I listened through the white noise of the transistor radio's limited reception (in a remote part of the Scottish Highlands, any reception is good reception) to the shipping forecast, one of the best ways of obtaining weather information, even for inland areas.

'There are warnings of gales in the following sea areas: Forties; Cromarty; Viking; Dogger;

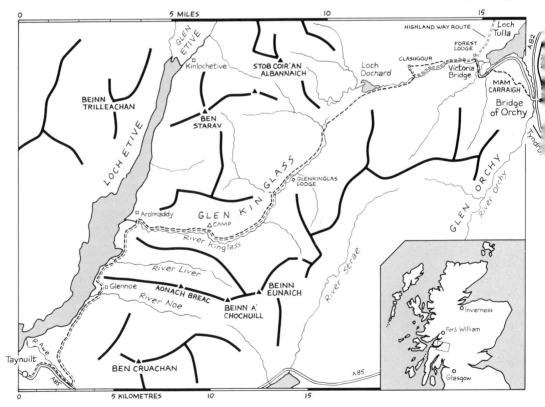

Fisher; etc.' We stared at the map, knowing that all sensible mariners would be ashore and all sensible mountaineers would be indoors.

On an outing with Edinburgh University Mountaineering Club in the late 1970s, we submitted our route which Tim had entitled 'A Glen Walk', which raised a few eyebrows in the bus. Many of the others would be up a mountain (feigning ecstacy) in any weather, or else in the pub. But for us, the natural routeway through the mountains, where the weather, though wild in every sense, was at least tolerable, was an equal challenge to scaling mountains whose summits held no view at all. To sit in the pub every time the weather was bad, we had decided, could be rather hard on the liver.

At the time, I had never heard of Glen Kinglass, but our walk through it was to be most memorable, despite the weather throwing its worst at us − right from the time the bus dropped us off at Bridge of Orchy until it picked us up on the Glen Coe road. Two days and two nights of being blasted by wind and storm had not proved comfortable, though enjoyable none the less.

More than a decade later, I listened to the same shipping forecast (I wonder if they do repeats of the most popular ones?) as I contemplated my departure on a similar trip but with three differences. First, I considered a more logical route would be to turn south down Loch Etive after traversing Glen Kinglass to finish the walk at Taynuilt. Secondly, the West Highland Railway was to be my carrier. Thirdly, on this occasion I was going alone.

As the train rumbled on its way from Edinburgh, first to Glasgow and then north along the West Highland line, the weather grew steadily worse. The squalls alternated with the stations on the many stops so that if the rain was off at one, it would be pelting down at the next.

'Tickets!' yelled the guard, as I looked at my return to Bridge of Orchy. It was very tempting to forget about setting out under these

On the Highland Way trail, near Bridge of Orchy.

conditions and take the next train back home − my ticket was good for any train during the next three days.

At Arrochar and Tarbet the train passed another of the 'Super Sprinters' going the other way. The doors open with the press of a button and I laughed out loud when its guard, standing in the doorway, did just that to find his tie streaming horizontally and his cap blown off an instant later. It was his good fortune that the wind blew it back aboard the train.

At Bridge of Orchy station, I bundled out of the train door, along with two other walkers − who had the good sense to make straight for the hotel. I donned full waterproofs and pack-cover and plodded on. The 'Bridge' of Orchy is a solid stone-built one, under which the River Orchy, the outflow from Loch Tulla, was in spate. Just as the road turned north, I took the footpath north-west, which is the West Highland Way route. The Way hadn't been officially in existence last time I did the trip, when we walked the five kilometres along the road to Victoria Bridge under the cover of darkness.

While I am a lover of backpacking and have backpacked the world over, I have my reservations about hordes of people all trudging through knee-deep mud, following a programmed route. Routes which provide a framework for visiting attractive regions, without confining the trekker to a rigid route or timetable, are surely best if they permit an element of choice as well as reducing the impact on the environment. In Scotland, where geographical constraints on the choice of route are relatively few, there is considerably more scope for variation than in many other countries.

The first few miles of path that wound over the shoulder of Màm Carraigh were a most beautiful beginning to the walk. I stopped to exchange brief words with a ranger wearing waders who was tending a stream that had overflowed its banks. Some aquatic masonry was being employed to help drain the ground which, through a combination of high rainfall and high visitation, can be very boggy for most of the year. He indicated that things being what they were, he expected to do quite a lot of stonework. He agreed that erosion quickly gets out of hand in the muddier sections, where each successive hiker tracks ever wider to avoid a muddy foot at all costs.

The Inveroran Hotel and its matchless setting.

Victoria Bridge.

At the high point, a cairn prompts the trekker to admire the view that stretches over Loch Tulla to Rannoch Moor beyond. I discovered another walker sheltering behind the cairn, trying to read his map before the wind flogged it to shreds. My first-series map failed to show much of the detail his second-series sheet included. Simon was from Liverpool and had thought better of an ascent of Beinn Dòrain in such weather, preferring a walk along a known path at a low level. We descended to Victoria Bridge and agreed to walk together up to Clashgour farm, beyond which lay the head of Glen Kinglass.

A weathered Right of Way sign pointed west at Forest Lodge. Here the West Highland Way continues north around the edge of Rannoch Moor — one of the toughest and loneliest sections of its 152km (95 mile) route. We watched two red cagoules several hundred yards away, bobbing along against the rugged moorland, no doubt eventually bound for Fort William. For us, there were trees for company (there had been a great deal of forest plantation since I was there last). The road to Clashgour had also been improved, and neither of us spotted where it departed from the riverside track. With our heads down and hoods up, we had been concentrating on the next two steps ahead to the exclusion of all else.

Back at the river (238421) Simon turned east as I turned west, glad that with all the rain, all the streams along the route were bridged. The succession of squalls with heavy rain and hail that descended were at his back, but in my face. But my suffering was made infinitely more pleasant by the apparition of Stob Coir'an Albannaich and other peaks of the Ben Starav group, which appeared snowcapped above the dark-grey cloud. The waterfall that forms the outflow from Loch Dochard tumbled down a granite outcrop, over which the path tracked a sinuous route. The slabby stone had accumulated much surface water and its associated flora made the rock very slippery. Falling on an outstretched arm, alone in a remote spot, I was reminded of the seriousness of commitment that the solo walker must make. There are fewer distractions when hiking alone; there is no pretence; nobody to argue with, but despite the scope for meaningful introspection, there is nobody to go for help. I picked myself up and continued more cautiously than before.

Despite my great determination to keep my feet dry (copious layers of snow-seal on the boots before leaving home; gaiters that cover the boots; taking a running jump over any soggy patch that threatened to exceed my normal stride-length), by this time they were well and truly damp. The most depressing thing about spending such a fortune on wonderful equipment, I decided, is that the more you use it, the faster it wears out.

Another rickety bridge spanned the river after my descent from the pass. It was a 'cross it and don't think about it' bridge and I wondered how many more years it would last. Two of the rusty steel cables had parted, lending a sensation of being in a big sea in a small boat. On the north side of the River Kinglass, the rough path became a 'Grade A' track. Completed in 1989, the construction of the road serving Glenkinglass Lodge has meant a temporary visual loss for the walker. But the stretches of the old track that I would see later, partly under the swollen waters of the river, would more than justify a well-levelled track with ditches at both sides.

For a while I was able to enjoy walking with my hood down and I was lucky enough to

witness a most spectacular striptease. Beinn Eunaich, frequently mistaken for the giant Ben Cruachan to the south, was tormenting me by revealing first one shoulder, then the other. The roving spotlights of sun beamed through the shifting cloud as if nature were putting on a light show. But when all was about to be revealed, the next squall hit and the grey curtains drew the performance to a close. Reluctantly, I put my camera back into its waterproof pouch.

The track down the glen was almost too good. On drier trips than this, I would have walked the river-bank in preference. I passed Glenkinglass Lodge on the far side of the river, a tidy-looking collection of buildings, whose resident guard dogs barked their welcome from afar. With a blackening sky and a watch that said 5 o'clock, I began looking for a suitable place to camp. The oak wood, 3km east of Ardmaddy Bay was not an ideal location, but provided more shelter than any other. I pitched the tent, with some difficulty in the rising wind, behind an old stone dyke whose boulders were covered in a luxuriant spread of moss.

The ground was lumpy and obviously poorly drained, but there was fresh running water only a few yards away. The babble of the stream was drowned out by the sound of the wind, and the odd gust would send the tent flapping uncontrollably. Intermittent showers with no bright intervals led me to expect that worse was still to come. I wanted to be well sheltered from north-west winds which would be very strong if the depression tracked through during the night. I used up the remainder of the daylight cooking, writing – and wondering if the tent would stay up.

The occasional crack of a twig outside and the hooting of an owl reminded me that I was not entirely alone. The wind had a roaring sound that seared through the valley to the west, forewarning me that a stronger blast was coming. I re-pegged the flysheet as taut as it

The wall of moss, Glen Kinglass.

would go. Outside, beyond the warmth and light of my little niche, the night was as black as coal. In the complete darkness, through the wind's howl, I thought I heard voices – a man's and a woman's.

'Who's there?' I yelled into the night, my words whipped away by the wind. Nobody was there. At any rate, nobody replied.

It was light by 6 o'clock but I dozed on for another hour. Putting the kettle on from the comfort of my bag, I noticed that the inside of the flysheet had been infested by a plague of black slugs. They were all over my pack, boots, stove and the tent itself. Delicious as I am sure they would have been, I chose tea and leftover sandwiches for my breakfast instead. I emerged from the tent to see that the cloud had dropped to about 150m. A fine rain was falling and the

wind had all but ceased. It was quite warm, which made sense as these were classic signs of 'warm-sector' weather. The depression had not tracked through. I was still in the middle of it. Unfortunately, this meant that all possibility of the mountain views could be ruled out.

Eight deer were grazing the grassy patches by the road. They allowed me to get quite close before I prompted their rapid departure by inadvertently snapping a twig underfoot. In my hurry to establish the tent the previous evening, I had underestimated the distance remaining to Ardmaddy. It took me more than twice as long as I had predicted. A quick look at the remaining distance to Taynuilt and at the West Highland Rail Guide convinced me to spur my steps. Momentarily, I was glad that the new route down Glen Kinglass cleaves the odd corner off the route of the old one, making it a quicker though harder surface for walking. Later, I found a long section of the old track under water. I rounded a corner to see ahead of me on a mound, a cairn and a lone pine tree. Lady Wyfold, the estate owner who died in 1976, was buried there.

At Ardmaddy I gazed out across Loch Etive, convincing myself that the faint blur separating two shades of grey was the far shore. The tide was high and the smell of the sea I had expected was absent. I continued across the bridge and up the track that led around the hill to Inverliver (which the local people spell 'Inverliever'). A decade before, I had turned north and walked first to Kinlochetive and then all the way to the Glen Coe road. The sound of an approaching vehicle made me turn around − a local estate worker offered me a lift in his jeep. I declined his offer, sensing that this was perhaps the most spectacular section of the trek. The smell of diesel hung on the morning air long after he disappeared.

Almost imperceptibly, the cloud had begun to lift and the land slid into sharp focus. A most spectacular series of views unfolded as the path climbed up the contours. I gazed down on the extended arm of the sea, which makes Glen Etive unique. It combines the majesty and desolation of neighbouring Glen Coe, with the mystique and delight of such sea lochs as Sunart on the west.

At Inverliver Bay a recently roofed house enjoys a most beautiful location. The deer in an adjoining field were not tame, they had just leapt over the fence to enjoy a more nutritious breakfast than available out on the hill. A 1m high fence, designed to keep twenty sheep in, is no obstacle for hungry deer.

Looking at my watch, I realized that my chances of making the lunchtime train were slipping away. It was frustrating being so warm in the constant drizzle, because there was no choice but to wear waterproofs. Walking fast simply made me wet from the inside instead. The path climbed up the contours and another section of imposing coastline unfolded. The spur, which descends west from Aonach Breac (096337), terminates abruptly in deep water, affording the most spectacular views up and down the loch. The settlement of Glen Noe was the last I was to see before the civilization that awaited me at my journey's end. The path wound right down to the shore after crossing the river and I was disappointed to see a large amount of flotsam littering the high-tide line. The massive amount of water that moves in and out through the narrow mouth of the loch generates very powerful tides. These can be seen in a most spectacular way at the Falls of Lora, near Connel Ferry, where the sea appears to flow like a river with large standing waves. However, tides that enable a waterfall to form in the sea are also quite able to transport floating debris dumped well out at sea into the confines of the loch.

I entered the mixed forest by the shore. It was sufficiently dense to preclude any chance of seeing the old granite quarry from the path. Granite was quarried extensively in the whole region during the last century and for the first part of this one, and transported by sea. But like many others elsewhere, the quarry closed when demand for stone could no longer justify the cost of its extraction. The road wound on into the forest. The trees were starting to show signs of spring − stubs of lime-green needles extended from all the darker branches. In the confines of the forest, I had no chance of seeing Ben Cruachan, which would force me back, perhaps in another decade, to try again.

A car purred up from behind and the lady driver offered me a lift. I was only one kilometre from the surfaced road, but closer to five from Taynuilt because I had to cross the bridge over the river Awe, some way upstream. I was quite sodden and my Achilles tendon had started to hurt. I thought about the train which was due in under an hour and what it would be like to be warm, dry and comfortable.

'Yes thanks,' I said. I made the train without difficulty.

THE ROUTE

A two-day walk over well-defined tracks. This 43km (28 mile) trek involves 520m (1,700ft) of ascent. OS sheet 50 covers the area.

The route from Bridge of Orchy to Taynuilt is a wonderful walk, with public transport at each end. The alternative, which I had done previously, is to walk north up Glen Etive to the Glen Coe road. For those with an aversion to walking on surfaced roads wearing boots (as I have), a more logical finishing point, subject to motorized transport being available, would be the point where the track to Coileitir (which has the bridge over the River Etive nearest the loch) meets the Glen Etive road at 137468.

The mountains of the Ben Starav range (to the north of Glen Kinglass) provide scope for day excursions from a base in the glen. However, because these hills are extremely rough and largely without paths, to contemplate a trek through them with loaded backpacks would be difficult. Similarly, the nearby hills of Glen Coe, though tempting for the traveller, are very steep-sided and, though criss-crossed by paths, are frequently treacherous in the wet, especially for those carrying heavy loads.

Knoydart Wilderness

When I was a boy in Scotland, I was fond of everything that was wild, and all my life I have been growing fonder and fonder of wild places and creatures.

John Muir

I drummed my fingers on the steering wheel, watching the temperature gauge needle climb into the red. Friday traffic was usually bad enough, but the holiday weekend had prompted even more people to take to the streets. With the frustration of a dual carriageway more closely resembling a car-park, tempers frayed,

horns blared and the occasional radiator reached boiling point.

For once, I was surviving the stress of driving in the city without resorting to my usual foul-tongued anger. Strangely enough, I felt at peace. I knew that as long as there remained one place where I could go — a place without roads,

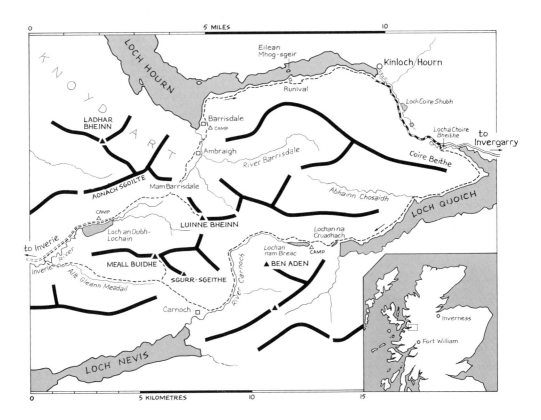

without people, without the artefacts and false values of civilization – the city could throw all the stress it liked in my direction, and I would let it all flow over me.

My vision of the place is clear – a remote peninsula on the west coast, where high craggy mountains meet the long arms of the sea; where the rough ground has been sculptured by ice, leaving a land surface of rock, water and bog, which, despite its harshness, is host to a large variety of animals and plants sufficiently tough to survive. This is a place where the westerly storms batter the living and the dead alike, occasionally flooding the rivers and preventing any possible escape.

Knoydart, as the tract of land north of Mallaig and south of the Loch Hourn is named, is synonymous with my vision of wilderness. Its terrain is rougher than anywhere else on mainland Britain, and, surrounded on three sides by water, its real charm results from its difficulty of access. Distances are irrelevant compared with other areas – while there are a few well-maintained paths, much ground is too rough to cross, particularly in wet weather when many of the streams are impassable.

The van was only a whisker narrower than the road which wound on like the coils of a giant snake, thrust upon the barren landscape. The group were queasy on the journey in from Invergarry – a distance of less than 18 miles which took us a little over an hour. The 4 miles remaining to Kinloch Hourn could wait until we had completed our circuit. After such a long drive, we were all anxious to get going on foot.

After the road left the shores of Loch Quoich, I persuaded the seventeen-seater brute to tuck into a passing place with minimal obstruction. Beside the first of four small lochans that dot the landscape between the loch and the sea, it was obvious that crossing the river was not going to be the problem I had anticipated. Firstly, it had been dry for some considerable time. Secondly,

a tumbled-down bridge, not marked on the map, provided a crossing at Loch a' Coire Bheithe (983036).

The group of nine established a slow trudge in the heat of the day, knowing that the first 5 kilometres were likely to be some of the roughest. We were fortunate, however, in that despite the lack of a path, the dry spell had all but completely firmed the succession of peat bogs. I had just finished saying to the group that the trackless shore of Loch Quoich would have been a purgatory in the wet, when I found myself knee-deep in bog, having punched through the dry crust. After the laughter died down, I threatened to put one of the more expendable individuals in front.

Rounding the peninsula and turning west, we

Crossing the Abhainn Chòsaidh.

were glad of the breeze now in our faces, that kept the midges away. All the streams that drain this rocky spur to the south were virtually dry, and the Abhainn Chòsaidh river crossing that has claimed lives in the past (966015) presented no difficulty.

A few hundred yards further on, we came to the path marked on the map. It seemed a remarkably well-built and well-drained one, and when we saw that it led directly from the loch itself in one place, we thought it must have been constructed to help build the dam at the western end of the loch and subsequently submerged when the water level was raised. This hunch was confirmed when a look at an old half-inch map dating from the 1930s showed the loch to be much smaller and the road to continue beneath the shore we had skirted. With half the effort,

we doubled our speed and continued round until we came to the dam itself. There we met a solitary hiker, bound for Sgurr na Ciche. Rather than follow him and the path, we chose to follow Lochan na Cruadhach and the stream that led from there to Lochan nam Breac, our campsite. This kilometre took us over an hour. The ground was wetter, more rocky and more awkward here, reaffirming my vision of Knoydart as a place of sheer ruggedness. We realized we would have been far quicker going the long way round and following the path on the south side of the rocky knoll that guards the eastern end of Lochan nam Breac.

In the bright sunlight of early evening, we set up camp on the level grass of the shore. The deer were obviously fond of the area as well, as evidenced by their footprints in the sand. The

The shore of Lochan nam Breac.

Lochan nam Breac.

waterfall that provided our drinking water was across the stream, though a series of stepping stones provided an easy way across (these are frequently covered over completely after heavy rain or in winter when the loch level rises significantly). There was ample driftwood for a camp-fire littering the shore, left after the higher waters of winter had receded.

A quick trip up the side of the hill allowed me to catch the evening light on the sinuous loch and the fiord-like landscape. Looking down at the row of tents, I was convinced that we had one of the finest campsites imaginable. From where I stood, the following day's route looked both inviting and challenging once it left the path beyond the western end of the loch.

I descended and showed the group how to make an ecologically sound camp-fire that would leave no trace. I have very mixed thoughts about fires in the wilderness, feeling that preserving the wild landscape intact is the most urgent priority. Too many individuals see a camp as being incomplete without a fire, and too many campsites in the Scottish Highlands are pocked with blackened circles ringed by charred stones containing sodden, unburned logs, broken glass and rusted beer cans. If fires are so important to outdoors people, then using low-impact techniques may be a more sensible approach to correcting the problem than imposing an unenforceable ban.

Using sand instead of rocks to 'wall' in the sticks, I created a lattice and put some of the dry grass that marked the 'high tide' line underneath for tinder. As the fire burns down, the sand walls can be advanced, reducing the size of the circle. This allows the remaining wood to be heaped up and each piece to be burned completely. The end result is ash, which is covered with sand, leaving no trace of the fire.

The group all agreed that it was important to make as little impact on the environment as possible, and felt that 'no-trace' camping not only helped foster an appropriate attitude to the wilderness, but could also allow many groups such as our own to visit an area without spoiling the feeling of solitude. Our discussion moved to camp hygiene and I told them of one beautiful campsite I had visited where we found spaghetti hoops at the bottom of the stream. I reminded them always to pour rinse-water out on to the land, where ants and other organisms could do the necessary on tiny food scraps. Contrary to some people's obvious belief that fish eat spaghetti hoops, I indicated that putting food scraps in the stream was akin to putting rubbish in the refrigerator.

The wind died away to nothing and the midges came out to find us. In response, we huddled closer around the fire, the woodsmoke keeping them at bay. A few stars twinkled from the darkening sky. The orange glow of our faces dimmed as the fire subsided. After the camaraderie of the gathering, the group dispersed into the darkness. It was a cold night.

The sides of Lochan nam Breac are so steep that the path climbs far up the hillside above the northern shore. We gazed down on the loch and the camp we had enjoyed so much. It was a picture that typified the very essence of wilderness, with nothing to indicate we were approaching the end of the twentieth century. But while we were privileged to enjoy it in our own company, our route was to lead us to the more frequently travelled parts of the peninsula and, considering that it was the holiday weekend, no doubt, scores of others.

We descended to the stream that formed the loch's outflow. It was barely a trickle, though the huge rounded boulders were obviously shaped by a most powerful torrent. For me, the most enjoyable part of the walk followed – a stretch without any sign of a trail, confined to the stream bed and boxed in by the canyon-like walls. But it was as subtle as it was imposing. The bright yellow marsh marigolds and bluebells decorated the way like a natural rock garden. These attractions combined with the

Morning vista.

challenging terrain to slow our progress considerably. After a while, we emerged at the flatter ground which marked the start of a path, none the worse for the experience. Again, I was reminded of the utter impossibility of this route in the wet.

Our path passed by a ruined croft and hugged the bank of the River Carnach. The cliffs that form the west spur of Ben Aden must have made a most spectacular backdrop for its former inhabitants, while several swimming holes further downstream would have made excellent bathing. The deciduous trees were conspicuous by their absence from the map, which seemed surprising to us as here were what were obviously the remnants of an ancient forest whose cover had once been more complete. However, having been given the task of making maps myself in the past, I remembered how difficult it is to portray objective criteria falling one million square metres of ground on 4 square centimetres of paper.

Despite the heat of the day and the desire of some individuals to go for a dip, we continued, knowing that our route ahead involved a climb up to nearly 600m. The twisting of the river seemed to extend the distance we had to cover, and having confused the two spurs that descend to the valley from Sgurr Sgèithe, we had overestimated our progress. The ruined chapel at Carnoch stood out from a considerable distance, marking the start of the climb to the pass of Màm Meadail. Thankfully, the path was a good one and the customary slow plod saw us to the top without stopping. It zig-zagged upwards at a gradient that was an effective compromise between hard graft and extra distance.

At the col we ate a belated lunch before making an ascent of Meall Buidhe. Having left our packs, the spring in our steps propelled us upwards quickly, though in terms of time, my route up a gully turned out to be more of a long than a short cut. Obtaining drinking water as high as possible was uppermost in my mind, but I had underestimated the route's difficulty. A recent rockfall had piled up above a narrowing of the walls and threatened to give way at any moment. Some careful scrambling saw us above it without mishap, though this was none too quick for the less confident. Once on the ridge itself, we realized that we would be overwhelmed by cloud before we reached the summit. As a result, I made everyone count paces to the cairn. As I have frequently discovered, the variation in the number of paces was considerably less than expected from the range in size of people in the group.

The mist cleared a little on the descent, and we were careful to avoid the gulley. The many vertical rock surfaces thrown up by the processes of weathering make Meall Buidhe one of the most treacherous hills in Scotland. We threaded our way between them, thankful that the mist never closed in completely.

At the Màm Meadail, we shouldered our packs once more and began the easy descent of Gleann Meadail. The path was a good one with a gradient that required little effort. Perhaps because of this, one of the group was lying face-down when I rounded a corner, having twisted his ankle. After all the technical difficulty of the canyon and the ascent, he had chosen the most easy, level section of path so far on which to fall. Gingerly and after some coaxing, he got to his feet. I went through a series of checks regarding how it happened and the positions of the foot that produced pain. If it was broken, then we could carry him to the pier at Inverie and send him to Mallaig on the boat the following day —

if not, he could continue more slowly with the group, bearing a lighter pack. The victim was somewhat concerned that I didn't want to see the ankle, but I knew that if we took the boot off, the swelling might prevent it going back on! He had been unlucky, and his lightweight walking boots which didn't quite cover the ankle, had allowed the foot to invert completely, causing ligament damage. I wondered if it would have happened at all, had he worn a more substantial pair of boots which came higher up his leg. The two adjustable ski poles that I had brought for assistance with river crossings were at last put to good use. With the level of the rivers so low, I was regretting bringing them, but they made excellent walking sticks (the manufacturer now makes a model specifically for walking). A longer pole for descents was particularly reassuring, though Jeremy's arms quickly became tired. Three of us took turns at carrying his pack like a holdall. It was exhausting work, and it brought home how well balanced packs must have been for us not to have noticed the weight they contained. We were glad that there was only a short distance to go before camp.

The path crossed the valley and wound down to join the Inverie river, though we saved a few hundred yards by using two old footbridges (not marked on the map) before the confluence. A large cross on a knoll opposite seemed strangely out of place, but it served as a guide to our progress. The wind had died away to nothing again, and the dancing cloud of midges that followed us ensured that any stops we made were brief. After reaching the main track, we ambled along towards Loch an Dubh-Lochain, determined to camp at the first flat ground we came to. This proved to be further than we intended — a small spit half-way along the north shore. A dead deer lay decaying in the heat of late spring and our shore was littered with what appeared to be the remains of a floating jetty. However, after ten hours of walking, neither of these blemishes was sufficient to force us to continue our search.

While two of our number braved the chilly waters of the loch, I looked at Jeremy's ankle which had swollen dramatically. While his supper was happily cooking itself on the adjacent stove, I had him sit on the bank with a foot in the stream and a towel over his head to keep the midges off. Though the others found this amusing, we all must have looked quite ridiculous, wearing Balaclavas for the same reason on a warm evening. At sundown there wasn't a breath of wind and the loch became as flat as a mirror. Beautiful as it was, we all retreated inside the dome tent, in a reluctant surrender to the midges before they made things too unbearable.

The awakening day was warm and the haze had disappeared. The climb up Gleann an Dubh Lochain the following morning was a treat. Once again the path was a good one and eased upwards at an economical rate, slowly revealing an expanding view of the mountains and coastline. Jeremy was making good progress with the sticks, the swelling having reduced in the night. Once again the sheer ruggedness of the terrain was impressive – an aura made all the more powerful by the sighting of a Golden Eagle riding the thermals far above. The cliffs of Aonach Sgoilte to the north, and Meall Buidhe's great rocky midriff to the south, appeared jagged and dark against an azure sky.

At the pass of Màm Barrisdale, we split up. I led a group of five up Luinne Bheinn (which we referred to as 'looney bin') while the three others walked down the path to Barrisdale. I had considerable difficulty in persuading Jeremy not to come on the climb! A series of four rocky haunches led to the top. Following an intermittent and indistinct path, we shot upwards, armed with only cagoules, cameras and chocolate, and hoped to be back at the col in under two hours. Like a fool I left my spare film in the pack. On what was proving to be one of the best days for mountain photography I've ever experienced, I had to choose which three shots to capture on film. The choice was agony – Rhum, Eigg, Muck and Skye were all visible to the west, while the hills of Kintail dominated the northern horizon.

We all marvelled at the view, recognizing Luinne Bheinn to be one of the best vantage points any of us had known. I was amazed at the effort it must have taken for my only previous ascent, some sixteen years earlier, when I had climbed both Luinne Bheinn and Meall Buidhe in a day from a boat we had sailed up from the Sound of Mull and had anchored in a bay at the foot of Ladhar Bheinn. I remembered feeling particularly bold because we climbed more than the height of the hills, our walk beginning at low tide.

The six of us descended carefully down the steep slopes to the packs, again grateful that the ground was so dry. At the pass we began the descent into Barrisdale – much steeper than the other side, and hard work. The path wound down into a birchwood (again not sufficiently dense to be marked on the map) and across the river. We passed the well-kept house at Ambraigh which enjoys views up five different valleys.

We passed the bothy at Barrisdale which seemed to be well maintained and well appointed. It worked on an honesty system, as did the neighbouring campsite. A note on the door indicated that a group from The John Muir Trust was staying there. John Muir, a man of great vision, came from Dunbar, east of Edinburgh, which he left aged eleven when his family emigrated to Wisconsin. His extensive exploration of the North American continent and his unfaltering conviction that the wilderness must be preserved led to the formation of the Sierra Club and the establishment of Yosemite National Park. The John Muir Trust, dedicated to preserving wilderness, has an active interest in Knoydart, and working parties regularly inhabit the bothy while maintaining the various trails in the area, to prevent erosion.

A herd of a dozen deer grazed the hillside, not 50 metres from the track. They seemed unperturbed by our presence, but wouldn't let us get any closer when two of us moved in with cameras at the ready. I learned that these had the habit of hanging around the bothy, preferring scraps left from various travellers to their more traditional diet.

We found the others flaked out on the beach in the mid-afternoon sun. With a rapidly flooding tide, the warm water in the lagoon behind the beach was mixing with cold and though any thoughts of a swim quickly vanished, we found the coarse shell beach underfoot as good as any foot massage. The paddle quite refreshed the feet after the pummelling they had sustained during the descent. Everyone was enjoying an easier day after the rigours of the previous one. It did not go unnoticed that some food was likely to be left over, and we all ate a second lunch. Nuts, raisins and sandwiches disfigured from their long journey were passed around. Dave slowly squeezed a tube of honey into his mouth until a gust of wind trailed it over his face.

There was a mood to that late afternoon, with the sun beating down and the sea breeze caressing our bodies, that belied our weariness. We were a happy bunch, all individuals working to a common cause, all sensing a closeness with each other and the environment. It was as though Knoydart had some special richness, born out of its isolation, that enhanced the experience. We counted ourselves lucky indeed, when we later discovered the area was nearly bought by the Ministry of Defence for military training purposes — a land-use incompatible with all other human visitation. A subsequent plot to franchise the land and sell it off as timeshares met with equally strong opposition, and we are fortunate that, thanks to associations like the John Muir Trust, the area will continue to be known as the wild, inaccessible peninsula it has always been.

We set up camp hastily as the wind died away to nothing, knowing the midges would soon make our task all the more difficult. Later, when the tide was rapidly receding over the sand bars of Barrisdale Bay, the warmer water did tempt some of us to go for a dip. With supper over, we entertained ourselves by expending some of the energy left after a shorter day. The highlight was our questionable performance of various Scottish country dances, simultaneously humming the tunes. Needless to say we had the campsite to ourselves! Even the deer left.

Summer was early. The sun set only a little north of west, yet the midges were out in their millions, heralding the wearing of Balaclavas once again and the rapid application of repellent. I lit an anti-mosquito coil which proved effective in keeping them away at first, but even this proved insufficient once the wind dropped. In haste, we dusted ourselves down, piled into the tent and zipped up the screen. We then dusted ourselves down again, realizing, to our dismay, that several hundred had entered with us. With military precision, Dave set about sequestering and eliminating every two-winged creature with a wet towel — antics which were made all the more hilarious by his total seriousness. Then the benefit of modern tents with two entrances became apparent. We were able to continue our merry-making safely from within the bug screens, while a through-draught ensured a flow of fresh air. This, our last night together as a group, was both a happy and a sad occasion. We were happy that our trip had been such a resounding success (even Jeremy agreed!), but sad that we could not have stayed longer. It would have been ideal to have had just one day without the hassle of moving camp, which could have been used equally well to climb Ladhar Bheinn or laze on the beach watching the tide rise and fall.

Supper!

Knoydart appetite.

The morning dawned cloudy. It was still and reasonably warm, but a higher humidity betrayed a possible change in the weather. I was eager to get the group moving, having a six-hour drive ahead of us later that day. I made my eagerness known with a shrill blast on my safety whistle.

The 10km that stretch from Barrisdale to Kinloch Hourn must rank as some of the most picturesque anywhere. There is a subtle combination of mountain and shore, with deciduous woods stretching up from the brown kelp and grey rocks of the shingle beach. The 'mule track', as it is sometimes called, is in very good condition and effectively minimizes environmental impact along this popular route into Knoydart, despite the greatly increased visitation of recent years. Though the path only ventures inland a short way, it climbs above the 100m contour, making some stretches quite steep.

Two pairs of nesting herons with young inhabited the Eilan Mhogh-sgeir across from Runival Bothy, and they could be heard from the path 500m away. The pungent aroma of the sea got stronger as we rounded the final bend to see the head of the loch and the signs of habitation that marked Kinloch Hourn and the end of our walk. The smell of woodsmoke mingled with that of the shore. A red post van purred away up the hill and into the distance. I contemplated the hour or so I would have to myself retrieving our van, while the others sampled the tea shop menu. As the path turned into tarmac, the sound of our footfalls was amplified as if to applaud our return to civilization.

The walk-out along Loch Hourn.

Leaving Barrisdale.

THE ROUTE

This four-day route would have been more enjoyable spread over five days. The total of 60km (37 miles) distance includes the 7km (4 miles) of road covered to retrieve the vehicle, and the 2,600m (8,500ft) total ascent includes both forays to the summits we climbed. OS Sheet 33 covers the area. Camping is not permitted between Kinloch Hourn and Barrisdale. An alternative route would be to enter Knoydart at Inverie via the ferry from Mallaig, which operates three times a week. From there, a route up Màm Uidhe, the valley to the north, leads towards Ladhar Bheinn. However, in addition to being equally as rough as the other mountains in the area, Ladhar Bheinn has few escape routes in bad weather, and the presence of magnetic rock on the north side renders the compass unreliable in places.

Exceptionally high rainfall in Knoydart means wet, boggy ground persists for much of the year, contributing to the erosion of paths, and making untracked routes a serious undertaking. In heavy rain, trekkers should either plan to stick to those paths with bridges or be prepared for a long wait.

Torridon by Night

I can remember vividly the estranged faces of my colleagues one Friday coffee-time, when I indicated that I intended to sleep the following night on top of a mountain without any camping gear.

'Worse than I thought' said one.

'Why can't you cut the grass or wash the car like any normal person?' said another. Yet, the more I tried to convince them of the virtues of an Alpine-style bivouac, the greater became their conviction that I must be seriously deficient in some mental capacity.

Torridon is not difficult to justify as a walking area. However, much more difficult is the selection of a single route that is able to convey to the walker the genuine wildness, remoteness and sheer rugged grandeur of the area as a whole. More than any other region in the Highlands of Scotland, my memories of Torridon are dominated by superlatives and extremes.

One April, my then fiancée and I were comfortably ensconced in our twinned sleeping bags, listening to the rising wind and rain battering down. The shipping forecast for most sea areas was for severe gales or hurricanes, and we were glad we had invested in a good

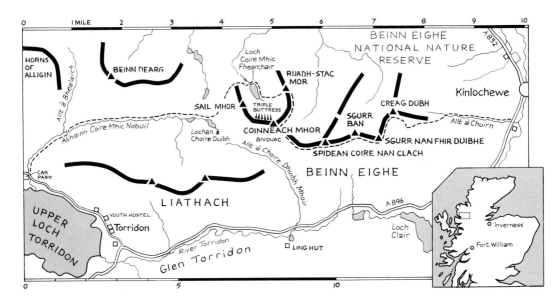

stormproof tent. However, in the small hours, after much commotion, two unwelcome chaperones (but good friends) bundled their way in from the blackness saying that their pegs hadn't held, the tent had collapsed and in the confusion, some of their belongings had been scattered to the four winds. Moira and I shoved over and, cramped as we were, the four of us sat round the stove avoiding the trickles of water that were exploring the flysheet floor. Content with a hot brew, we beat a hasty retreat to the car at first light.

In August, when I had plucked up sufficient courage to return, my brother and I enjoyed four days' magnificent mountain walking, staying in the relative luxury of a camper van. We exposed film after film at the spectacular scenery for which the north of Scotland is so famous. But when the wind dropped, we discovered to our cost the severity of the Scottish midge whose plague was in full flight. I have heard many estimates of how long the little blighters survive, from hours to days, but however long it is, it is too long! We ate, drank and breathed them, scratched, squashed and smeared them, our eyes stinging from a chemical which seemed to be more of an attraction than a repellent! Perhaps it is significant that the Torridon store sells mosquito nets that are worn over the face!

The majority of walkers or mountaineers either camp or stay at the Youth Hostel (or alternative bunkhouse accommodation) and sample the delights of the area by daytime forays in a variety of directions. While there is considerable justification for this, my objectives were somewhat different in planning a hike through the area. I sought to combine the scenic rewards of several day trips on one route, but quickly saw that a single route over all the big peaks would not be practical. Firstly, linking the mountains together is very difficult owing to their adversely steep and loose rocky flanks, combined with the roughness and wetness of the moorland in between. Secondly, the land

separating the hills is eroded down to such a low level, that the walker would have to lose a great deal of height between any two. Indeed it is this that makes the area so spectacular — the surrounding valleys have been scoured right down to their rocky basement of gneiss, leaving huge and distinct mountains in relative isolation.

The challenge was to select a route that involved climbing one mountain or ridge, but offered such impressive views of the others as to reveal the true character of the area. After much deliberation, I came to the conclusion that an extended traverse of Beinn Eighe from below Beinn Alligin to Kinlochewe best achieved this objective. This route — some 22km (13½ miles) long and involving 1,400m (590ft) of ascent — would take between eight and ten hours. With midsummer rapidly approaching, I concluded that it could be most enjoyably accomplished as an overnight excursion with a high-level bivouac during the few hours of darkness that separate the long days of a Torridon summer.

There are many benefits from undertaking a trek overnight. On this occasion, I was aware that summer was early and that the midges were approaching their normal July concentrations before the end of May. A high-level halt in the more chill air of the ridge top, if not the likely speed of its prevailing wind, could guarantee us freedom from the pests. There were the usual logistical concerns of a five-hour drive, and how best to use the time remaining on the day of arrival. There was the quality of evening and morning light, which, for the photographer, mean the portrayal of a landscape (which in some photographic conditions appears flat) in something more closely resembling three dimensions. There was the very considerable advantage of ease of movement in the absence of all the encumbrances of normal camping gear that are both bulky and heavy. Perhaps the most positive benefit of all, however, was the assurance of solitude that being up a remote

The Abhainn Coire Mhic Nòbuil.

Liathach boulderscape.

mountain during the night entails. Walkers were returning to civilization as we left, and in a contentment that spurred our methodical steps, we plodded outward as the great mountain giants lengthened their shadows.

We had left the car a little after 5 o'clock at the car-park three kilometres west of Torridon village (869576). We had elected to take the 1:25000 Outdoor Leisure map covering Skye and Torridon, rather than the three 1:50000 series maps which, through no fault of their own, meet along the route. While I welcomed the great detail which the larger scale map portrayed, and that satisfying sense derived from crossing a large expanse of paper in a short time, I regretted that the contours were not metric, and found that the excessive rock detail

frequently obscured the pale contours, making them hard to interpret. However, the rock detail is more than justified, as after we crossed the footbridge over the Abhainn (river) Coire Mhic Nòbuil just above its junction with the Allt a' Bhealaich, the landscape became more of a 'boulderscape'. The inviting path leading to the horns of Alligin led north, while we continued east along the riverside path. The U-shaped valley showed the signs of extensive glaciation – rocky till, drumlins and other glacial debris were strewn everywhere as if the ice had only just retreated (which it has, in geological terms). The rough peat and heather make cross-country travel a chore, and the general rocky surface to the land will no doubt have disappointed many campers who sought

Lochan a' Coire Dhuibh.

flat ground. Nevertheless, we found three tents along the path, tucked away neatly between boulders.

The path gained height at a very slow, steady rate and at Lochan a' Choire Dhuibh (930597) we were surprised to discover that we had climbed more than 300m. We left the path here, cutting across the rough hillside to the lower of the two paths that led north and into Coire Mhic Fhearchair, often quoted as the most spectacular coire in Scotland. While the boulders and bog forming the path allowed marginally swifter travel than the surrounding terrain, it demanded all our attention. Luckily, we were in no hurry.

Two pairs of climbers descended the path from the coire during the evening. They had been doing rock climbs on the Triple Buttress, the major crag of the area. We continued up to the waterfall, where the loch's outflow cascades over a spectacular rock apron, peppered with boulders of assorted sizes. The Torridonian sandstone forming the bedrock was a deep red colour, contrasting sharply with the white quartzite that formed the summits of most of the mountains.

'DAAAAAAY-O' I yelled, having established that nobody else was within earshot. Several seconds of silence passed before the echo came back with astounding clarity. The sound reverberated half a dozen times before it finally subsided. Discovering the child in us allowed us ten minutes of rest and laughter. Four deer grazed nonchalantly on, no doubt thinking, 'Bloody walkers and their bloody echo!'

The stream that feeds Loch Coire Mhic Fhearchair links a series of three rocky pools. A rough path follows the stream, terminating in a rock-chute that leads directly up on to the ridge. The deer were on one of several grassy patches which appeared to allow easier access to the shoulder of Ruadh-stac Mór, the highest point on the Beinn Eighe massif. We continued upwards, the deer keeping their distance of

Coire Mhic Fhearchair: one of the finest glacial cirques in Britain.

twenty yards or so ahead of us, until they retreated north to pastures new.

A bank of descending cloud threatened to obscure the sunset we had hoped for. We hurried on, furtively glancing back at regular intervals to compare our progress with that of the weather. Resting on the brilliant white stone of the summit, we had sufficient time to enjoy the glassy waters of the Minch and the mountains of Harris before they disappeared. Fortunately, our grasp of the local geography was sufficient for us to put a name to most of the hills. Also, I was reminded that here the landscape and light can play a trick, convincing the observer that the sea slopes towards the land. This is because the rock basement, while appearing flat from above, is tilted at a slight angle. After four hours of walking, no doubt our tiredness accentuated the effect.

With the approaching mist already having capped the twin peaks of Liathach, we pressed on, the damp and cold catching us by surprise in the still air. We descended to the col where it appeared most walkers gain the ridge via the rock-chute and continued up Còinneach Mhór. The cliffs of Triple Buttress seemed steeper when viewed from the side. We continued east and found a luxuriant spread of flat grass that was ideal for a bivouac. We had taken plenty of fluid with us, but this site was even served by its own spring. Its flow was clearly intermittent, the water barely running on this occasion. However, water on any ridge is a scarce commodity, and had we been thirsty, we would have used purification tablets and filled our bottles — far and away preferable to old corn snow that persisted in the cracks, grey and speckled with its resident flora and fauna.

By 10.30 p.m., the cloud descended lower. Content that we had the optimal bivvy site on the entire ridge, we were well satisfied with our lot. Nevertheless, an eerie silence prevailed as we watched the clouds form and disperse before our very eyes. One by one the neighbouring peaks vanished, leaving us to our island of grass amidst the advancing sea of silver. This powerful visual effect, combined with our general tiredness and the leaching of the colour from the land and sky sent us both off into a deep sleep.

At 4.30 a.m. it was silent, bright and clear. The rain had stayed away and although the outsides of our sleeping bags were a little damp from condensation, they remained comfortable and warm. We enjoyed the pleasure of breakfast in bed before packing up. Again, the effort associated with packing up a bivouac is negligible compared with that of striking camp. Two minutes after draining the flask of lukewarm coffee and having a bite to eat, we were

treading the white quartzite pebbles of the path and beginning our traverse of the ridge.

While there was still no wind, the omnipresent cloud was damp enough to make conditions quite cool. The movement of air flowing across the ridge at various places teased wisps of cloud from the dense mass above. Though a little lower than Sàil Mhór at the westernmost end, the summit of Beinn Eighe itself was to be our highest point on the main ridge by a grand total of 1m. Nevertheless, the trig point is not on the summit, but on a small subsidiary top to the west. It was here that I set up the camera for a self-timer shot, when my exposed film rolled out of the camera case, narrowly missing falling into the cylindrical hole in the trig point's centre. Annoyed that my carelessness had nearly cost me the record of the previous sunset, I stowed the exposed film in a pocket of my rucksack.

Frequent glances over our shoulders told us that the cloud was following in our footsteps. It appeared that we were at the junction of two weather systems, about to be overtaken by cloud and rain. To the north and west, cloud boiled over and around all the hills. To the south, wisps of cloud licked over into the still air where a glassy Loch Clair was visible far below. Having heard that the old Scottish Mountaineering Club Guidebook suggested a rope for the ridge ahead of us, I was keen to press on while visibility remained. While we had no rope, I felt happy that it was the exposure rather than technical difficulty that was the prime concern. Like so many previous ridge walks I had done in the past, the exposure is considerably less intimidating when the mist is thick!

Before we lost much of the height between Beinn Eighe summit (Spidean Coire nan Clach) and Sgurr Bàn, the mist had overtaken us. It was important to maintain our concentration and pace ourselves for the remainder of the climb, taking full advantage of any momentary clearances

Beinn Eighe seen from the east at Kinlochewe.

to have a good look around. Like the pinnacles of Liathach, the notches scalloped into the section of ridge linking Sgurr Bàn and Sgurr nan Fhir Duibhe to the east, are very exposed and loose. The path takes a dive below the ridge to avoid these, though in good weather, they are well worth a few moments of airy scrambling for those not averse to having air on either side. The mist swirled between the spires which appeared like great fangs, lending an aura of excitement to the ridge that only Glen Coe and Skye can offer elsewhere in Scotland.

A momentary clearance once again revealed the hills of Kintail far away to the south, with their ribbons of snow reflecting the early light. To the north was thicker cloud again, and a spectacular glimpse of Slioch was shortlived. Our footfalls broke the otherwise perfect

silence, and the pebbles rang with an almost metallic sound. Alone in the clouds, it would have been easy to convince ourselves we were in Spitzbergen or Patagonia.

At Creag Dhubh, the final summit of the ridge, we stopped to search for a trace of the path. Thinking there may be several routes off the hill, I fully expected there to be a division of the path here, but was somewhat disillusioned to find that it came to an abrupt halt. We intended to track south and pick up the path that followed the stream and led into the Beinn Eighe National Nature Reserve. Given that many walkers intending a traverse of the ridge would choose this route, I expected a path to connect the summit to the Reserve path. However, in the less-than-perfect visibility, we found no trace of it, and committed ourselves to

Towards the eastern end of the ridge – the elusive path down to the Nature Reserve.

Looking backwards towards Sgurr Bàn.

a 300m descent of loose scree. Descending loose, unconsolidated rock can often be a great pleasure, but if it is too loose or steep, or has a precarious run-out at its base, it can be treacherous. Before starting down we laced our boots tightly to give extra ankle support and prevent any tiny stones from working their way in. We took great care to avoid one another's fall line in case any dislodged stones picked up sufficient speed to cause an injury. On a previous descent, years before, I had propelled a meaty pebble at high speed squarely into my brother's back. His pack took the brunt of it, but in the windy conditions that prevailed then, he did not heard my yells of 'rock' and 'below'. In our present state of tiredness, it would have been all too easy for a careless or unlucky foot placement to set a rock in motion. Large groups are particularly at risk, not only producing far more airborne missiles, but also providing a bigger target. Happily the two of us escaped without mishap.

The visibility improved once more and we traversed back on to the shoulder, finding the path that had eluded us. I cursed the cloud for obscuring it, cursed my eyesight for not being what it used to be and cursed myself for being too lazy to make a thorough enough search. It stands to reason that the shortest and most logical route connecting two points is a straight line.

At the spring line we enjoyed a long drink of fresh water. At a time when the majority of the population was still horizontal and unconscious, we devoured our second breakfast. But we didn't tarry long — we had noticed the warmth with our loss in height, and as soon as we stopped, the midges found us! We continued down the rocky spur to the edge of the forest. Here, the spur terminates in a steep drop to the stream, and the edge of the Nature Reserve is marked by a deer-fence. The Beinn Eighe National Nature Reserve is one of the foremost Reserves operated by the Nature Conservancy Council. The combination of conservation with public education appeals to the growing number of visitors who visit the Reserve each year. A sign indicated that poor land management had largely been responsible for the demise of the natural forest cover over the last 300 years. A large section of valley was fenced off in order to keep out the red deer in an attempt to regenerate the forest. While we applauded the concept of natural regeneration, there seemed to be little evidence that young trees were becoming established. Deer devour the tender saplings and must be kept out if the forest is to be allowed to survive. At the end of the last ice-age, the vast majority of the Scottish Highlands was covered by such forest, but since the clearing of much of the land for farming, together with the introduction of new species, the natural balance of the ecosystem has been irreversibly altered.

White posts indicated points of interest for a nature trail, but without its accompanying literature, we didn't know what the posts referred to. The sweet waters of the Allt a' Chuirn gurgled away, while a number of Highland birds which we took to be Crossbills, sang their welcome to the new day. We were almost down and with my quadriceps aching from the long descent, I contemplated the 18km (11 mile) run that separated me from the car. I have often found people to experience greater soreness when descending than when ascending, a fact attributed to the increased load the working muscles must bear, generating tension yet at the same time being lengthened. Uncharacteristically, they were complaining, and my first few paces of the run confirmed that the heavy lumbering feeling was not my imagination.

With such a limited amount of traffic on the road, the chance of a lift was slight. Moira stayed to guard the packs, resorting to walking back and forth to keep the midges away. This unpleasant interim reinforced our pleasure at our high-level bivouac. What a night it must have been in the still valley for the poor campers, and what a feast the two-winged blighters would have had.

I got a lift for only a fraction of the total distance. A van from the Scottish Conservation Group was full of young workmen who were mending the path behind Liathach that we had walked the previous evening. It made me happy to discover that yet another dedicated group of individuals was working to preserve the wild character of the land by minimizing the impact of increasing numbers of visitors. The thought of these tough individuals labouring in the hot, still conditions made those last few twists of road slip beneath my weary feet a little more easily.

THE ROUTE

Depending on daylight hours and fitness, a single-day traverse of our route — 22km (13½ miles) long, 1,400m (4,590ft) of ascent — is a realistic prospect. A post bus service operates on the road from Kinlochewe to Torridon which may assist in retrieving a vehicle for those with more sense than to embark on an 18km run at the completion of the trek. My experience is that the midges can be bad here during late June, July and August. May, September or October are preferable. Winter traverses would be a very serious undertaking indeed, requiring the full array of winter mountaineering skills.

A shorter route would be to avoid the longer walk to the north of Liathach, and commence at the other end of the same path (958568) marked by a ruined cottage and a car-park. The Ling Hut provides bothy accommodation nearby (958563) while Torridon village has a Youth Hostel and a campsite. Bunkhouse accommodation is available at other locations in the glen.

Midsummer at Cape Wrath

The stone landed with a dull thud.

'Your lie', shouted Steve above the roar of an incoming wave. The sand was soft, and our stones sank deep into their craters. Steve walked back and made his throw. It came to rest a few inches to the left of the jack. It was obvious that he had clinched that end.

The wave had spread itself as far as it was able and was now on its way back out. The delightful sound of its outgoing, with the accompanying reflection of the evening light, prompted a pause in our game. The cross rips (the currents that flow at an angle to the direction of oncoming waves) can be a hazard in a big surf, though today they were small. When the sand was bare once again, we collected up the balls and began another end.

'Pétanque' or 'Boules', as the game is known, is a most natural way of passing the time in such an idyllic location as Sandwood Bay on Scotland's remote north-west coast. The equipment for our game comprised several well-rounded stones and a flat expanse of sand. Because of this, we considered it highly possible that neolithic man had invented the game, and played it right where we stood, thousands of years ago. The only drawback would have been the compelling view that threatened to distract those, ancient or modern, who undertook the pastime with less than complete seriousness.

We had chosen well. While there were millions of smooth stones on the river bed, almost without exception, these were flat, like bars of soap. But on a cursory exploration of the camp environs, we found a vertical gash in the rocky headland, whose base contained stones that approached perfect spheres. The continual turbulent action of the waves within the confines of such an environment allowed a much more uniform weathering, that had resulted in perfectly fashioned stones, as if they were made by the most skilled of craftsmen.

Steve had been a generous winner, allowing me to score far more points than I deserved. Three throws each, with the closer person's throws counting one point for each stone, the game could reverse the fortunes of its players in an instant. Despite its requirement of the utmost concentration, the game took little energy, and we whiled away several hours as the sun slowly sank into the north west.

'I'm lying two', said Steve, 'Your last throw needs to be good.' I concentrated on the target, swung my arm back and released the stone ball, backward-spinning, in a high trajectory.

'Too bad, I win!' said Steve, with some thinly disguised criticism of my technique. I had run out of excuses for failing to produce my winning shot when I needed it most. Not only did Steve go on to win the game, he won all the games. Coming second was something I would have to learn to accept.

Although several hours of daylight still remained, Steve and I were tired after the long drive north. We had chosen the route via

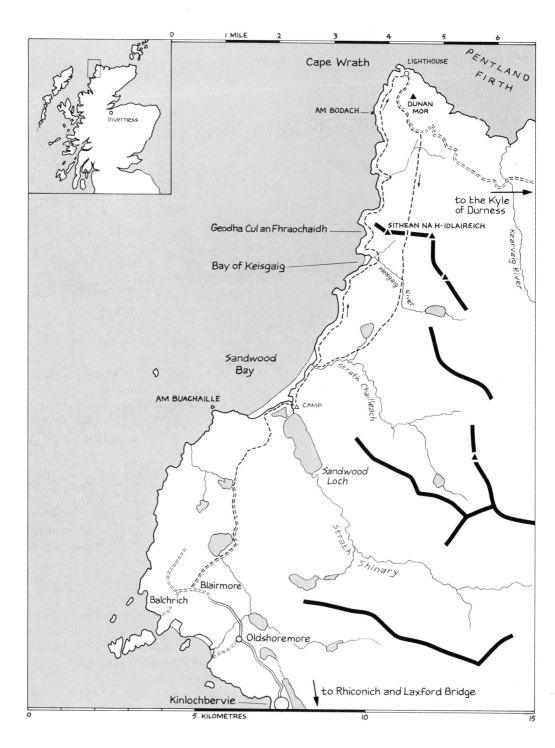

The bothy at Sandwood Loch.

Ullapool, which involves an extra 18 miles (30 km), but saves the extended section of single-track road that crosses almost the entire breadth of the country from Bonar Bridge to Kinlochbervie.

The wind, such that there was, blew gently from the east, with the result that most locations on the west coast were well sheltered. On the walk in, the banks of white bog-cotton in bloom barely moved in the still air. The day was bright

101

Approaching Sandwood Bay.

The beach at Sandwood.

with powerful sunlight through the haar, and with the approach of midsummer, the sun was high in the sky.

Three figures appeared on the beach. They were trekkers from New Zealand who, like us, were bound for Cape Wrath the next day. They were particularly taken with the two rocky outliers that the pounding surf crashed over, which provided excellent vantage points for wave-watching. We joined them, on the condition that they joined us for a game of *boules* afterwards.

Two hours later, we had triumphed over our antipodean friends, and retired to our camp. It commanded a view of the entire bay, from atop a dune just to the north of the short stream draining Sandwood Loch (225654). While there

were more than a dozen tents within ten minutes' walk from our camp, most were concealed behind dunes for shelter, or clustered down on the flat grass by the lochside. We were more concerned about the need for sufficient wind to keep the midges off, and had good reason to be proud of our choice. Earlier, while the occupants of other tents were sampling the anaesthetic sensation of bathing in the open sea, a small herd of free-range cattle nonchalantly wandered across the river and started grazing the more lush grass by the lochside. An alarmed group of schoolchildren sent the cattle off in the direction of any tent but their own, antics that left the cows most confused, and Steve and I well entertained as we ate our supper.

With a hearty meal inside us, we had made a thorough exploration of our camp and its environs. The shallow freshwater loch is connected to the sea by a short river which flows over a broad expanse of sand and pebbles. Its course had obviously changed since the map was made. A score of sand dunes crowned with tufts of grass guarded a lagoon, beyond which lay the beach and the silvery sheen of the sea. Perhaps most spectacular of all was the black index finger of warning that stood to the south — Am Buachaille, a magnificent sea stack. Here was a great collection of landforms that inspired awe. But today, this stormy corner of Britain, fashioned by the extremes of nature, was host to an almost perfect calm.

A faint orange glow in the sky became a powerful red light as the sun appeared from behind a bank of cloud. As the crimson orb poured out its gold on to the lagoon, the incoming waves resembled a lava-like flow of apricot. Sensing an opportunity not to be missed, we ran down to the beach, cameras in hand, hoping to capture something of the occasion on celluloid. The sun assumed its customary flattened shape and within a couple of minutes it had slipped below the horizon. Colder instantly, we returned to the tent. The bright sun, which we expected to rise in the small hours, ensured that we didn't sleep in.

The following day we were awoken not by the sunlight but by the tuneful sound of a skylark.

Sandwood.

Sunset at Sandwood Bay.

Sandwood. (Photo by Steve Senior.)

The soporific effect of the northerly air had ensured that we were well rested. It was already warm and bright by the time we were ready to leave, though with such a magnificent camp, we were almost reluctant to be on our way. Although we could see in the far distance the lighthouse at Cape Wrath itself, we knew that several hours were to pass before we would reach it.

We exited over the rocky knoll to the north of the river draining the loch, and halted to examine again the weird configuration of granite and gneiss that had been folded like links of giant sausages. We quickly realized that the 9km (5½ miles) as the crow flies between us and the cape would involve nearly double the distance of walking. With the limited resolution offered by the inland relief, fixing our position along the clifftops was tricky. As usual, we had overestimated our progress, our eyes the only part of us able to follow the crow.

The second stream we came to — draining Strath Chailleach — had half a dozen tents at its mouth. The inhabitants, young schoolchildren, had the northern tip of the beach to themselves. (It is effectively sealed except at low tide when it is possible to walk around the headland.) After a brief chat, we left them to their morning ablutions and continued north.

The highest cliffs of the walk soon appeared — an impressive rock wall of red sandstone, 150m (490ft) above a surging sea. Despite the sun's angle being too high for perfect photographs, we couldn't resist the temptation to capture what we could. After all, there was too much to see further on for us to stay put and wait for the light.

Steve was a photographer of some considerable note. I hoped to glean something of his expertise over the course of the walk, having admired the product of his labours for more than a decade. He had with him one camera body and three lenses — a 28mm wide-angle, an 80-200mm zoom and a special 500mm telephoto that reflected the light twice before it reached the film. As a result, our shared pack was not as light as either of us would have hoped.

While my auto-zoom lens worked very well, automatic cameras in general don't give the photographer much information — they just get on with the business of taking the photographs, winding on for the next one as soon as the first is taken. I saw the benefit of Steve's equipment directly affecting the picture — he rotated the polarizing filter covering his lens as I focused on the sea, far below. The result was a greatly improved clarity in the colour and considerable detail of the sea bed — not only something I had never photographed, but something I had never

Wave watching.

seen before. I also learned of the need to under-expose slide film on such bright days, and doubly so when shooting into the sun or over water. Steve also had a hood to shield the lens from a refraction effect for shots towards the sun. The lack of a tripod was not a problem on such a bright and still day when shutter speeds were sufficiently fast to remove the risk of camera shake.

We approached the Bay of Keisgaig. Here two streams, both very low, converge at the foot of a broad chasm. As a result, we lost nearly all the height we had worked to gain. A ruined shieling with the remains of a sod roof stood near the confluence. It was hard to imagine how anyone could have eked out an existence in such a place, with barren soil making farming difficult and mountainous seas making the launch or recovery of a small boat (to say nothing of a fishing vessel) a fearful prospect.

The south-west facing spur of Sithean na h-Iolaireich terminates in impressive cliffs to the north side of the bay. We edged closer to the drop-off, gingerly craning over in anticipation of the view. Despite my years of climbing, I was dumbstruck at the airy feeling of the extreme exposure — something that had long prevented me from doing any rock climbing routes on big walls. With a strong sense of self-preservation, I declined Steve's challenge to see who could throw a stone furthest out to the sea.

The rocky apron to the north of the spur was more impressive still. With bright sunlight burning down on the red rock, parts of it resembled the Grand Canyon in Arizona, particularly a stone chute which will make short work of walkers unfortunate enough to lose their footing on the path at its top.

The next inlet, Geodha Cul an Fhraochaidh, is equally impressive. A series of rocky spires, each resembling stacks of coins, juts out into the bay. On top of these are rounded boulders, clearly the work of none other than Mother

Bay of Keisgaig.

Nature herself, arranged into neat piles. I jogged round the arcing headland while Steve remained to provide scale for my photograph. There is a real danger of losing the sense of scale in pictures that lack such a reference, despite it being overwhelmingly obvious in the field. For the benefit of providing scale in my picture, Steve stood, contentedly, atop a knife-edged spur with a sheer drop of over 120m (390ft) to the sea on both sides. If photography is the objective, trekking partners need to be of bold disposition.

Another kilometre to the north, we approached the canyon cut by the nameless river that presents a major obstacle to an easy route north. We successfully descended its eastern end and followed the stream west for a few hundred metres. The ravine was sheltered and seemed to amplify the roar of the sea. Following the rocky river bed, we kept glancing up, half expecting a giant tidal wave to be bearing down on us. Before long, we found a suitable grassy slope that avoided the looser rock, which we ascended easily. However, both of us agreed that in wet weather, the canyon should be protected by secure belays and a rope or, better still, avoided altogether.

Cresting the haunch of the lower hill to the north, we were somewhat dismayed to find yet another stream to cross and a further hill to climb before we reached our objective. With the same black top to the lighthouse peeping out over the shoulder of Dùnan Mór, it seemed little closer than it had hours earlier.

The impressive views of the stack of Am Bodach were a consolation. Nearby were several large caves, into which the incoming waves disappeared. I imagined how impressive they would look from the water level, but feared my limited skill in a sea kayak would mean that such an excursion would be highly questionable. We looked up to see a couple of day-trippers coming the other way and knew we were getting close to Cape Wrath itself.

Significantly, the wind had increased. I doubted the capacity of the Pentland Firth to be as still as the sea to the west. It is a notoriously rough stretch of water owing not only to the unceasing wind, but its very powerful tides, as anyone who has taken the short sea crossing to the Orkney Isles will confirm.

The lighthouse (and more particularly the foghorn) is built right on the very edge of the cliff, an edge that should not be approached by those who suffer from vertigo. While the stack to the north-west is spectacular, the mainland cliff is absolutely vertical, and looking down its edge to a heaving sea is not something I am keen to repeat. In the biting wind at the clifftop, we donned windproofs, reminding ourselves why lighthouses are round, and why, in a storm anywhere in the Highlands and Islands of Scotland, it may be unwise to camp in the lee of a wall. After nearly four hours of strenuous walking, we tucked into our sandwich lunch, admiring the gulls soaring effortlessly on the thermals, at times barely an arm's length away.

While just a kilometre north of John o' Groats (Duncansby Head), and south of Dunnet Head, we had, without question, reached the remotest corner of mainland Britain. The lighthouse was the only habitation, and a disused gun outpost on the hill suggested the strategic importance of the place during the World Wars.

Our route back was something of an anticlimax. It became hot as soon as we left the cape, the shimmering air and bright sun leaching the colours from the landscape. While the coast would have been equally spectacular in the reverse direction, we took an inland route that was more direct and involved less ups and downs. We had to be careful to avoid the military area to the east, occasionally used for bombing practice (a friend was warned off more than a decade previously, while an unexploded shell was searched for, located and then detonated).

The Lighthouse at Cape Wrath.

We met the New Zealanders, still north-bound, half an hour after we had left the cape. They were exasperated that the apparently short journey had taken them so long. They had begun along the coast, but had cut inland in an effort to save time. They indicated that the lack of fresh water had caught them off guard, resulting in parched throats and dehydration. However, despite the dry weather, we managed to find sufficient running water to keep our bottle topped up for the entire journey.

The difference in rock-type has a most profound influence on the appearance of the land surface. Where the gneiss is at the surface, a great density of rock outcrops prevails, all with weird and wonderful textures. However, the Torridonian sandstone appears to result in few outcrops, and the smooth terrain that results, hosts a deeper soil.

As to whether the glaciers scoured deeper where the gneiss is revealed, or whether the junction between the two is more complex than it appears, we were uncertain, as no doubt are many of the geologists who travel from far and wide to examine the rocks here.

Wearily, we trooped into camp, after failing to round the headland because the tide was in. It would have been a great end to the walk to have completed the last section in bare feet, the sea soothing away any discomfort. But we couldn't be sure of the water depth at the headland, and we were a little concerned about the quicksands, about which we had heard plenty but had seen little.

The good weather was coming to an end. Despite our fears for rain, we were able to enjoy a succession of mugs of tea and our supper outside, after which we strolled down to the beach. Although we had invited our Kiwi friends for another game of *boules*, neither of us expected to see them, judging by how they had looked at the cape. After three more defeats, I suggested we climb on to one of the rocky mounds for some wave-watching.

With the tide now well out, the two rocky outliers could be easily accessed. Clefts in the rock result in a skyward jet of spray which, if caught by the wind, is liable to soak all those nearby. We watched the sets of waves with their almost hypnotic charm. Sets of five, six, seven or even ten were common, separated by periods of relative calm. The delightful sound of the outgoing backwash, terminated by the breaking of the next incoming wave, made a cacophony, while the green walls of water that exploded into white spume surged against the dark rock with a force that had the less confident scurrying for the security of the beach.

There was no sunset – only the seemingly endless light of midsummer and the perpetual action of the waves. But as we stood, we sensed that the mood was changing from the peace and calm in which our brief visit had fallen, to something more akin to and deserving of the name 'wrath'. While we both longed to be witness to a storm battering this lonely shore, such statements are more easily made in good weather, or from the safe confines of an armchair by the fire.

THE ROUTE

Our three-day trek involves 38km (24 miles) and 960m (3,150ft) of ascent. (Our route stuck rigidly to the coast and considerable savings of distance and height could be made by cutting a few corners.) Sandwood Bay offers the most spectacular camping of the area, though plenty scope exists along the streams further north. Official campsites exist at Oldshoremore (210587) and Balchrick (183601).

To get to Blairmore, the start of the trek, follow either the A838 (via Lairg) or the A894 (via Ullapool) to Laxford Bridge. From there, follow the A838 to Rhiconich and then the B801 to Kinlochbervie. A sharp right turn off this road before it descends to the harbour area leads to Oldshoremore (208586) and the start of the trek near Blairmore (195600) where a sign to Sandwood Bay indicates a two-mile drive and a two-mile walk. Despite the extra distance, I was glad that we had left the car at the end of the track, as it is particularly rough and passing places are few.

A daily minibus service runs in summer from the passenger ferry across the Kyle of Durness (370660), taking visitors to Cape Wrath. This could assist the logistics of returning to a vehicle, or alternatively, the campsite at Durness.

Much of the area on the north coast near the cape is owned by the Ministry of Defence. While military activities do not prevail all the time, the restricted area is well marked on the map, and should not be entered.

Practical Considerations

While backpacking is undoubtedly a pastime for young and old the world over, it is important to draw attention to some characteristics of backpacking in Scotland that differ from backpacking anywhere else – aspects which may contribute to enjoyment of the unexpected, but which equally may punish the unprepared.

The wild land of the Scottish Highlands is not to be feared, but it must be respected. While many other parts of the globe have predictable climates, Scotland's is precisely the reverse. Walkers should know what to expect and be prepared for the worst. Many potential hazards exist – some within our control, some outwith it – that may greatly influence our safety and enjoyment. Unfortunately, inexperienced walkers may only recognize a hazard when it is too late to avoid it. On the other hand, experience under difficult field conditions can be very valuable – in particular, bad visibility that requires precise compass-work to find a safe route. Deciding to make for the nearest café rather than the nearest mountain when the weather is unsuitable will undoubtedly lead to frustration, though such weather is by no means rare. Adopting a plan where routes are flexible enough to be modified is frequently the best solution – one that I use myself all the time whether leading groups or hiking on my own.

The paths in this backpacking guide vary greatly in quality, but several of the routes, particularly the ascents of mountains, involve covering broken ground that is frequently steep, wet or even hidden beneath snow! As a result, much of the equipment required may be rather different from that used for long-distance walking overseas. Access to the land – particularly for camping – cannot always be guaranteed. Knowledge of when to expect difficulties can avoid disappointment or even confrontation.

SCOTTISH MOUNTAIN WEATHER

Scotland is well known, and by some well loved, for its fickle climate. The fact that the Scottish Highlands have the capacity for extraordinarily severe weather during any month of the year demands great respect and careful planning of the backpacker. For some, probing the thick mist with a compass in driving sleet is a picture of hell; for others it is simply another facet of the backpacking experience. Having four seasons in a single day at least carries the assurance that boredom is unlikely to be a problem during any highland sojourn. What follows is a very generalized overview of Scottish weather. For a more scientific and comprehensive account, refer to Further Reading.

Unfortunately for Scotland and its inhabitants, it lies at the junction of two great air masses – the Polar and the Maritime. This junction, a north-east to south-west line known to meteorologists as the Polar Front, plays host to a single phenomenon which, occurring repeatedly, characterizes the weather for much of the time — the depression. These commonly develop from irregularities in the circulation of the atmosphere when a wedge of polar (cold) air from the north, pushes into the maritime (warm and moist) air to the south. This creates a 'wall' of warm air which sweeps north, pivoting around a wall of cold air which sweeps south. These walls are referred to as fronts. An anticlockwise cyclonic circulation develops around the junction of the fronts, resulting in a drop in air pressure. As a result of the forces of the global circulation and the rotation of the earth, depressions almost always track west to east towards Scotland, though they may move north or south to a limited extent. Depressions evolve with time, interact with other weather features (including other depressions) and eventually become inactive and disappear. However, it would be wrong to suggest that the pattern is always this simple.

Associated with depressions are a variety of weather patterns. These, in turn, vary according to how well-developed the depression is when it reaches Scotland. Some may reach Scottish shores while still developing and wreak greater havoc over continental Europe or the North Sea, while others become occluded before they reach us.

Cold fronts are characterized by heavy squalls of precipitation with fierce wind gusts. Warm fronts are characterized by low cloud, continuous drizzle and low visibility. During the life cycle of a typical depression, the cold front moves faster than the warm front, overtaking it and forcing the warm air upwards. Occluded fronts, as they are called, may be warm or cold, and tend to travel more slowly than the fronts themselves and usually reflect the characteristics of warm or cold fronts respectively.

All this makes the weather conditions at any given time difficult to interpret by the lay observer. However, it is possible to make use of the three-dimensional nature of depressions, where the wind at the ground surface level blows in a different direction from that at a higher level in the atmosphere. The movement of the lowest clouds in the sky will be roughly parallel to the isobars (lines joining points of equal pressure). The uppermost clouds will be blown in a direction similar to the track of the depression. By using careful field-observation, backpackers may see the signs that indicate the general position of the depression relative to themselves, in the absence of any forecast information whatsoever.

An observer facing away from the wind who sees the upper wind appearing to blow from left to right, can expect the weather to deteriorate; if the upper wind appears to be blowing from right to left, then the weather is likely to improve. Any individual in possession of an altimeter (which measures air pressure and gives a height equivalent) is able to predict the general trend of the weather as well. If the apparent height increases, the weather is likely to deteriorate; if it decreases, the weather is likely to improve.

The heaviest rain and strongest wind is normally associated with a cold front, while the poorest visibility is normally associated with a warm front (or the warm sector behind a warm front). While families of depressions frequently travel sequentially in a similar direction, each successive one tends to be south of its predecessor. During winter the Polar Front moves south to a position between Florida and south-west Britain. While many depressions track well to the north of Scotland during the summer months, in winter, Scotland is directly in the line of their normal path.

The opposite of a depression is an anticyclone. This is a region of high pressure which is usually associated with stable conditions and good weather. Light winds circulate clockwise around the centre (in the northern hemisphere). Two principal types are recognized — one in which the cold air is confined to the surface levels (cold anticyclone) and the other, where it is confined to upper levels (warm anti-cyclone).

Cold anticyclones are common in winter where cold air sinks and spreads out, bringing cold conditions to the whole of Britain. Warm anticyclones affecting Britain frequently arise from the Azores and comprise convergent winds at high levels. These result in extended periods of clear weather.

During the relatively stable conditions of an anticyclone, it is possible to witness one of the most spectacular features of the weather, not just in Scotland, but anywhere — temperature inversion. This involves cold air draining down into the valleys overnight and sinking below its dew point (the temperature at which water will condense), forming cloud and leaving the less dense, warmer air at higher levels. The result is that the backpacker who camps high up is frequently rewarded with the pleasure of gazing down upon a sea of cloud through which the mountains are poking their tops. With the heat of the sun, the colder air in the valleys warms up, evaporating the moisture and 'dissolving' the cloud, usually early in the day.

In the Scottish Highlands, the effect of mountain relief on weather is considerable. The same scenery that holds equal attraction for the backpacker and tourist, has a profound effect on temperature, precipitation and wind speed. General forecasts of weather do not take account of this effect, underestimating the severity of mountain conditions.

Precipitation

With most of our prevailing weather arising from the west, it will come as little surprise that the west coast is considerably wetter (nearly five times) than the east. As a rough guide, the west coast may have about 300cm (118in) of rain per year, and this decreases by 5cm (2in) per year for every three kilometres travelled east. However, the mountains themselves attract considerable precipitation as a result of their height, forcing the air-flow to rise into the colder temperatures higher in the atmosphere. The resulting condensation forms cloud, and commonly rain. This accounts for the annual rainfall at the summit of Ben Nevis (Scotland's and Britain's highest peak), being more than double that of Fort William, the town at its base, over 1,200m below. A great deal of precipitation on Scottish mountains falls as snow during the winter months.

Wind

When an air-flow encounters the barrier of a mountain range, it is forced to accelerate over or around the obstacle. This accounts for the very significant increase in wind speeds observed with increasing height on the Scottish hills. All mountainous regions of Scotland can encounter very strong winds. These may vary according to the prevailing weather conditions and be 'funnelled' by local topography, producing wide variations. Saddles at the junction of valleys assist the backpacker who wishes to camp high by providing flat land on an otherwise sloping terrain. Unfortunately, these sites are frequently as windy as the summits. Because general forecasts do not take account of such local variations, it is often very difficult to predict how windy conditions are likely to be. However, the automatic weather station permanently sited on the summit of Cairngorm records wind speeds which are relayed in certain weather forecasts including a 24-hour service available by phone.

Temperature

The schoolchild who questions the fact that hot air rises, has probably experienced walking the hills. It seems perfectly logical that the mountaintops should be balmy if the Physics teacher has told the truth. But the reality is that because nature is so complex, the schoolchild (and most other people for that matter) has little hope of understanding any more than simple generalizations. As air rises, for whatever reason, it expands because of reduced atmospheric pressure. This process draws heat from the air and has the effect of cooling it. In Scotland, the effect is normally 1°C lost for every 150m height gained (cloud cover reduces the severity of the cooling with altitude). Another effect is that a point on the lee side of a mountain is frequently warmer than a point of similar height on the windward side. This is particularly relevant in winter when temperature may affect the stability of snow slopes.

It is quite artificial to separate out all of the components of Scotland's mountain weather. In reality, the effects combine to increase the severity of the prevailing conditions alarmingly. The wind chill is the effective cooling power of the wind and temperature combined. A 20kph (13mph) wind blowing at 10°C (50°F) is equivalent to still conditions of −40°C (−40°F). While air temperatures seldom reach very far below freezing, wind speeds on mountain summits frequently exceed 100kph (60mph). When precipitation is introduced as well, the situation becomes more serious, and adequate clothing and sensible route choices become paramount.

Without doubt, the best way to become conversant with the vagaries of the Scottish weather is to combine regular outings to the hills with all the forecast information available.

HAZARDS OF THE HIGHLANDS

Knowledge of the causes of the hazards, together with effective action may avoid accident or injury. While the mountains hold malice for neither backpacker nor beast, safety can never be guaranteed in any mountainous terrain. Whether the walk is for a week or a single day, it is up to each adult individual to make a sensible route choice according to fitness, knowledge, experience and prevailing weather conditions. Safety is concerned with being realistic with this choice and having an appropriate attitude and responsibility to modify the choice as conditions dictate.

While certain hazards occur independently of the action of the individual (exo-hazards, or objective dangers), such as lightning or avalanche, it is the ones that do involve individual action (endo-hazards) that are more serious in the Scottish Highlands. Directly or indirectly, the weather can be seen to be the source of virtually all the hazards that the backpacker may encounter, but perhaps man's greatest danger of all is himself.

Avalanches

For the trekker who enjoys braving a Scottish winter, a basic awareness of avalanches is desirable. Only on the walk in Ben Alder country did I encounter an avalanche slope, but in more severe winters with heavier snowfall, the pattern could be very different. Because they are relatively rare, avalanches are frequently overlooked by outdoor enthusiasts. While avalanches in Scotland are neither as large nor as spectacular as those in higher mountains, accident statistics show them to be a serious risk when they do occur.

The cause of avalanches can be attributed to instability in the snowpack, arising in many different ways. Recently after a fall of snow the snowflakes may settle, reducing the maximum angle of repose; the crystals themselves may undergo a change of structure (metamorphism) that leads to weaker layers supporting accumulations above; meltwater may truncate the 'anchor-layer' that holds snow on to a gully or rock face; a cornice (an overhanging section of snow or ice produced by strong wind-blown snow), may collapse, triggering the snowpack below to slide. The list of possible causes is long and many of the factors may operate simultaneously.

The most dangerous slopes tend to be at angles greater than 28° and facing away from the prevailing wind. Here, weather forecast information (and weather history) is a valuable addition to field observation regarding how the slopes are loaded. A snow pit may show if weak layers are present in the pack, and its sides may be probed by fingers/ice-axe/ski-pole for hardness.

While evaluating the risk (safe, marginal, unsafe) is a technical judgement, the decision whether or not to cross is a moral one. A group should have a probe (a ski-pole) and a shovel with them, to effect a search if the slope releases and buries one of the party. The group should cross one person at a time and everyone should be closely watched while they are doing so.

In the unlikely event of the slope releasing when an individual is only partly across, he or she should yell out, and the observer should mark the last seen point. While it is often possible to climb or slide out of an avalanche, instinct will tell the individual to try to stay on the surface, thrusting a limb above it if possible. If searchers see no visible sign of the victim, a search must be started without delay, sweeping a fan-shaped area below the last seen point and keeping a vigilant watch for more slides. Often pieces of equipment will leave a tell-tale trail to the victim. Rescuers should block-search the fan-shaped area, probing 70cm (30in) apart until the victim is located. Unfortunately, if the victim has not been found in the first hour, the survival chances are less than 50 per cent. Going for help usually means recovering a body. For a detailed textbook on avalanches, refer to Further Reading.

Cold Disorders

Cold disorders include frostbite and hypothermia. Thankfully, frostbite is very rare in Scotland, where multi-day excursions involving camping on snow are the exception rather than the rule. Instances of frostbite have occurred during bad weather when day walkers or climbers have been caught out overnight unintentionally, without food or shelter. Hypothermia is a common year-round phenomenon with a great number of contributing factors.

Frostbite refers to the freezing or part-freezing of body parts – most commonly extremities such as fingers, toes, ears and nose. When excessively cold, the body conserves its heat by shutting down the circulation to such peripheral areas. Ice crystals develop in between the cells of the tissue which, with continued chilling, enlarge and cause damage to cell membranes and capillaries. This effect is made worse with tobacco smoking or dehydration. Previous sufferers are more likely to get frostbite than others. Symptoms include a sensation of coldness (numbness in more serious cases), white skin and pain. An old treatment involving rubbing the affected area with ice simply compounded the damage. While the recommended warm bath treatment is of little help to the hiker out in the wilderness, it is important to note that thawing should never be attempted if there is a serious risk of re-freezing again. Neither direct heat nor alcohol should be applied, and any blisters that form should be preserved intact. Prevention of frostbite centres around having suitable equipment, keeping comfortable and well hydrated, and checking for signs of pallor in the group before the more serious symptoms have a chance to set in.

Hypothermia is a very common and serious problem in Scotland. Maintaining the body's heat balance, constantly striving to keep its equilibrium of 37°C (98.6°F), must weigh the insulation value of clothing and heat produced from exercise (and the intake of foodstuffs) against the heat lost by the wind, wet and cold temperatures of the environment. In inclement weather the body's heat balance may be in equilibrium because individuals are able to exercise at a high enough intensity to generate sufficient heat. However, the balance will change very rapidly when exercise stops or slows, for instance when encountering a steep hill or reaching the crest of a ridge. Aside from wind, wet and cold, fatigue is the fourth factor that may predispose an individual to hypothermia. Ironically, stopping to assist one individual alters the heat balance in the entire group, so it is important for everyone to put on extra layers of insulating clothing.

Frequently, a situation may arise where the body may not be able to work hard enough to keep the balance. If this occurs, the temperature of the body will begin to fall, and if the process continues, hypothermia will result. With continued cooling, symptoms of violent shivering, nausea and cold are replaced with muscle rigidity, severely impaired co-ordination and incoherence. Extreme cases of hypothermia frequently involve a paradoxical sensation of warmth, followed by unconsciousness, which, in the absence of rapid medical assistance, commonly results in death.

As long as the symptoms are recognized early enough, hypothermia is reversible by treatment at the time. The main priority is to remove the victim from the environment of heat loss. This may mean descending to a valley, digging a snow-hole or erecting a tent. At the same time, a vigilant eye must be kept on the victim, with constant reassurance. Once some form of shelter has been organized heat should be introduced via another person and, provided the victim is fully conscious, some easily-digested food or a warm drink should be administered. (Beware of hot drinks which can burn the victim's mouth and throat.) If possible, dry clothing or a sleeping bag should be used for insulation and any wet clothing should be removed. Modesty is no reason not to climb naked into a sleeping bag with a stranger when lives are at stake – even when both sexes are involved! But just in case anyone is in any doubt, this is not the time to declare amorous intentions! Any re-warmed victim is predisposed to becoming hypothermic again, owing to a reduced capacity for heat generation and an altered blood chemistry.

One major problem with hypothermia lies in recognizing the symptoms in ourselves. I used to think that all outdoor instructors were immune until I got hypothermia myself! Adequate shell clothing is a must for all, and those leading groups should carry an emergency bivvy bag and extra food. However, even this can be insufficient. Victims' packs frequently contain all of the necessary items for survival, and in many cases, deaths could have been avoided if individuals had taken sufficient time and care to keep comfortable by making use of the things they carried with them.

Heat Disorders

Heat disorders are comparatively rare in Scotland. Heat exhaustion, when the body's core temperature rises above 37°C (98.6°F) is reversed with cool drinks, rest, shade and cool immersion. Under such conditions it is vital to keep adequately hydrated. However, it is important to remember that under such conditions, a stream on a map may be dry. Snow patches may provide water on ridges well into the summer, though the wind-blown dust may necessitate purification to render it safe. Sunburn may occasionally cause extreme discomfort, particularly when the individual's pack is chaffing at the shoulders. As much as 80 per cent of the sun's rays can penetrate through cloud. Often when you notice the sun, it's already too late! Adequate protective cream or lotion should be applied before going out.

Animal Attack

I remember having fallen through the ice on the way to the ascent of a frozen waterfall and narrowly missing an avalanche the same day, only to be savaged by a farm dog on my return to civilization! Domestic pets apart, Scotland must be one of the few places where there is a lack of dangerous animals for the walker. (Backpackers often take dogs with them, though these should be kept on a leash near farms and under control at all times.)

Talk of adders on Highland moors is mostly that — these creatures have a natural fear of man, and sightings are extremely rare. Of much greater concern is the Scottish midge (a tiny insect which can wreak devastating havoc in just a few minutes). A still day in July or August anywhere in the Highlands (particularly in the West Highlands) usually brings them out in their millions. They darken the sky with their presence and render the pleasures of wild camping a positive purgatory (I have seen them hanging like seaweed on a naked arm). The solution is to avoid the height of summer for camping at low level in the valleys, unless it is windy enough to keep them away. Walking is not usually a problem, but the walks mentioned in this book are not intended to be done without stopping! A full bottle of repellent should be part of every hiker's summer kit. Avoid damp places when looking for somewhere to camp, and if the weather is good, camp high, where there will be a few million less.

River Crossing

In this book, the routes where river crossings are likely to be a problem are in Glen Tilt and Knoydart. Refer to Further Reading, though the following notes may prove useful.

Before setting out, check the route for any unbridged streams. Streams wider than 8m (26ft) are represented on Ordnance Survey maps by a double line. Scout the stream thoroughly before deciding on the best place to cross. Collapsed bridges are seldom safe places as rusting cables, etc. may be submerged. While streams may reduce volume if followed upstream, flatter terrain near lochs will see a stream widen. However, flatter terain provides a safer crossing place. The fastest flowing current and the deepest channels are usually towards the outside of bends. A good exit is essential and steep or loose banks should be avoided.

With groups, more confident members should ferry loads for the less confident ones. A log or ski pole makes a useful 'third leg' for individual crossings. However, in deeper or faster water, the group may be better crossing together. I have found that the most suitable technique in many cases involves forming a line facing upstream, parallel with the river's direction of flow, with the biggest person at the upstream end. A close grip of the person in front's hips and a co-ordinated movement produces the minimum resistance to the water. Individuals should continue to face upstream, with the leader edging sideways so that the team 'ferryglides' across. Legs should not be crossed over, as this frequently causes stumbling. Hip belts should be undone, in case an individual does fall in — it is better to let the pack float for a few hundred metres than to have its owner suspended face-down in the water.

The last thing is to remember that you do not have to cross! It may be safer to retreat the way you came in or to wait for the level to drop. If the terrain is steep, or the surrounding rock is impermeable, then the rivers will not only be quick to rise, they will also be quick to subside after the rain has stopped.

EQUIPMENT

It is difficult to do justice to the enormous subject of equipment in the limited space available, but highlighting the most urgent priorities may prove useful. Firstly, it is important to realize that choice of equipment is largely a personal matter, and that inadequately equipped backpackers do not always perish! But while we are often allowed the grace of learning from our mistakes, the important items must not be neglected. Of these, shell clothing which is both wind and waterproof, and footwear are paramount.

Polyurethane-proofed material, neoprene-proofed nylon, oiled cotton, or Goretex are all examples of shell clothing. The usual dilemma is sacrificing breathability for waterproofness. As most people are aware, everything works reasonably well when it's new, but the real test comes when a few good hard seasons of wear and tear are put in. My personal preference is for Goretex now, though I was 'converted' several years after many colleagues. I had had bad experiences with it leaking, failing to work at sub-zero temperatures and becoming clogged with dirt very easily in the past. However, the manufacturing processes have been improved to the point where I now use it most of the time. Fears of delamination are allayed if the garment carries a two- or three-year guarantee (remember to keep the receipt in a safe place).

I prefer a smock design that pulls over the head, because it can be used for skiing or cycling as well. Hikers who do neither of these may prefer a longer design and a two-way zip down the front. I also carry overtrousers, which I only use 'as a last resort'. These could be sacrificed in summer if weight is crucial, though I generally carry mine none the less. The breathability of Goretex is not perfect, and I have noticed that the area of pack in contact with the back still produces the typical patch of perspiration on the back of the shirt — the earmark by which walkers can be recognized world-wide. Goretex needs a through-draught or slight air pressure differential, inside to outside in order to work, and I have heard some people report that their age-old frame rucksacks allow the waterproofs to breathe more effectively.

Boots are essential for walking in Scotland. While low-level walks on good tracks can be completed in running shoes in good weather, awkward, badly drained ground needs the stability that only boots offer — particularly when a heavy pack makes its bearer less stable. Training shoes may be taken to relax in around camp, though many times I've taken mine and not used them owing to wet weather.

Boots that are best for use in Scotland will be waterproof. The breathable varieties with mesh uppers are to be avoided. While plastic boots are becoming more popular, I prefer a one-piece leather boot with a traditional vibram sole. Some newer lightweight boots on the market with soles that are rounded at the heel offer poor grip when descending snow or wet grassland. While weight is undoubtedly important, boots designed for all-year-round use must be sufficiently rigid to take crampons. They usually have a steel shank that is half or three-quarter length, adding significantly to the weight. Comfort is fundamental, and so many varieties are available today that everyone should find a pair that fits reasonably well.

Packs or rucksacks must reflect the duration of the trip. They have changed most dramatically over the years, external frames having been almost completely replaced by internal ones. My only advice is that you buy a sufficiently big pack to allow everything to be put inside. Sleeping mats, commonly the largest item, can be rolled into a tube which lines the entire pack. If the pack is too small, packing it will take care and patience, and when you need your waterproofs, gloves or insect repellent, they are sure to be in the least convenient place. My packs are all internal frame ones with adjustable sides which can take skis, and they have lots of pockets. Many people use a large bin-liner bag to keep the items inside dry (I have yet to see a 'waterproof' pack keep its contents dry in a good downpour), but I prefer to use a waterproof pack cover made from neoprene-backed nylon, which has the advantage that the pack itself remains dry. Virtually all modern packs have a well-padded hip belt. On some models it is necessary to loop the webbing through the buckle twice to prevent it from slipping. I have found the hip belt to be the most suitable place to carry a camera — it is readily accessible and doesn't batter the chest with every stride. (When disconnecting the hip belt it is important to remember whether a camera worth several hundred pounds is strapped to it.)

Tents are at best a compromise between size, utility and weight. Newer tents with fly-sheets that come right down to the ground are to be recommended, and other features such as double-entrance doorways or a self-standing capability for use on snow, are desirable. When buying a tent, remember to check that the bug screen is sufficiently fine to keep out the midges!

It would be all too easy to go through the merits of all outdoor equipment, but such a protracted discourse could take up the whole of this book. Gear choice is highly individual, and what suits one person, may not suit another. With the baffling array of equipment and products on the market nowadays, it is easy to spend a fortune. Temper enthusiasm for fashion or gadgetry with common sense, and if you go to a reputable equipment outfitter, the advice will be free.

Physical Fitness

Backpackers do not need to be super-athletes. A certain minimum of fitness, however, will ensure maximum enjoyment of any expedition. In the choice of what you take with you on each excursion, you make an assumption of what your body is capable of. It is possible to save weight in every item of equipment, but being physically strong enough to bear a moderately heavy load is even more important. Adequate fitness — particularly cardiovascular (heart-lung) fitness — contributes not only to success and enjoyment, but provides a margin of safety in case of the unexpected. Continuous activities such as brisk walking, running, cycling or swimming are best for providing the type of conditioning leading to enhanced cardiovascular fitness.

I do not consider walking the outdoors to be the right arena for either an intense fitness programme or a weight-reducing diet. Rather, you should go to the outdoors with a clear impression of what your abilities and limitations are and plan an excursion within them. Pushing the limits of your capabilities too far during a walk, particularly for the inexperienced, is to invite misadventure.

Contrary to popular belief, profuse sweating does not mean a lack of fitness. Men sweat more than women, and fit people sweat more than unfit people (though the fact that men sweat more than women does not imply they are fitter). Individuals who are prone to sweating must take care to minimize perspiration-condensation-dampening of clothes, which significantly reduces their insulation value. Modern outdoor underwear helps 'wick' moisture away from the skin, allowing evaporative cooling and enhancing comfort. Adequate fluid intake is vital if fluid loss through sweat is significant.

It is important to recognize the considerable difference between day walks and carrying full packs over the same terrain. For walkers unused to carrying more than daypacks, the demands placed on the body may cause discomfort or even injury. Calf muscles frequently tighten up after steep ascents while long or steep descents, where the individual is continually checking the pack's desire to plummet earthwards, may precipitate stiffness or soreness in the thigh muscles. Descending involves much greater impact on the joints of the body. Those with a history of ankle or knee injury may be predisposed to complications unless sufficient care is taken. Adequate leg strength, such as that which can be provided by weight-training or cycling, will provide some protection for such individuals.

The right type of food for long-distance walking must be balanced against its weight and its ease of preparation. Sensible eating should not be totally forgotten when planning a trip. Vitamin J (junkfood) intake should not be allowed to dominate the diet! Some foods (for example margarine or cheese) don't travel well and are best taken in a tube. Convenient meals are usually those ready quickly. If cooking times are short, this saves on fuel as well. After a long day, perhaps the last thing you will want to do is to baby-sit the stove for an hour. Light-weight foods need not be bland.

With walks of up to a week, malnutrition is unlikely to surface. The greatest nutritional need is likely to be carbohydrate and I regularly use quick-cooking pasta, bulgar (cracked wheat) or rice for the base of meals. A visit to the local wholefood store usually reveals goodies such as almonds, cashews, dried fruit, onions, peppers and even dried tomato purée which can combine in any permutation to form the garnish. I usually load an empty film tub with a potent cocktail of herbs and spices to ensure that the results are anything but bland.

You should use your kitchen counter as a lab-bench for testing an assortment of recipes before you leave home. That way, if you don't like what is for supper, you only have yourself to blame.

Lastly, if fitness means a sound heart and lungs, adequate strength, flexibility and co-ordination, and a healthy diet to boot, you must endeavour to maintain a balanced life-style with a reasonable level of activity all year round — our bodies do not thrive on neglect and healthy year-round activity helps us adapt to the rigours of any new physical challenge.

ACCESS TO THE LAND

Considering how much of the wild country of Scotland is privately owned, yet publicly used, there are very few incidents arising from a conflict of interests, and even fewer prosecutions. The fact that Scottish law recognizes no definition of 'trespass' has been, and is frequently, used by visitors to claim a right of access. However, regardless of whether access to private land is intentional or not, or whether damage is caused, a landowner may be within his rights to ask the visitor to leave and is entitled to use reasonable force in doing so. Dogs, if taken, must be under strict control, and prudence must be exercised when near livestock. Of particular concern is where to park the car or van before starting a trip. Many places exist for legal parking of vehicles, but with dramatically increased numbers of visitors, it is very important not to obstruct access for local traffic or to park on a private road, gateway or entrance.

Section 3 of the Trespass (Scotland) Act, 1865 makes camping and lighting a fire on or near enclosed or cultivated private land or a private road without the permission of the landowner an offence. However, the Act refers to 'those who encamp' which targets those who camp for extended periods in one place. The essence of backpacking is to move from one place to another and if the camp is gone in the morning, it is far less likely to cause antagonism. Ecologically sound camping practice and maintaining a spotless campsite are essential if confrontations are to be avoided.

Most access problems — certainly the most emotive ones — arise during the shooting, or stalking season. The private estates make a large percentage of their income at this time, and irrespective of the views of the backpacker on the subject, the right of estates to deny hillwalking access must be respected. But shooting will never be continuous in any area, and checking with local estates is always a good idea. They usually recognize the need for groups to camp overnight in remote areas. The more remote the place you want to go, the less the potential there will be for access difficulties.

Backpackers who are unclear as to their rights should seek permission by enquiring first to the Scottish Landowners' Federation, or reading *Heading for the Scottish Hills (see* Further Reading).

Glossary

Note: (g) refers to a derivation from the Gaelic.

alt or allt (g) stream

arête snow ridge

bealach (g) saddle or col, often a pass

bearing direction of the compass

bothy mountain hut or shelter

cagoule waterproof jacket, originally with no front opening

cairn pile of stones, often but not always marking route or summit

coire (g) cirque or cwm – steep wall or hollow forming head of glen or valley

col saddle or bealach

contour line on map joining points of equal height

cornice overhanging snow ledge

feldspar silicate mineral, a constituent of granite

glen (g) valley

klister soft and sticky wax used on ski soles for touring

midge tiny biting insect, prolific in Scotland

Munro Scottish mountain over 3,000ft (914m) high

pacing counting steps to measure distance for accurate navigation

rut mating season of the deer

schuss downhill glide on skis

self-arrest use of an ice-axe to control or stop oneself during slide (on steep snow or ice)

shieling (g) remote dwelling, originally at high summer pasture

snow-hole shelter excavated/constructed out of snow

till undulating land surface associated with glacial origin

windslab compact and cohesive snow type produced by wind action

Further Reading

Barton, B. and B. Wright, *A Chance in a Million — Scottish Avalanches* (The Scottish Mountaineering Club, 1985)

Cliff, P., *Mountain Navigation* (Book Publications, 1986)

Langmuir, E., *Mountaincraft and Leadership* (Scottish Sports Council and Mountain walking Leader Training Boards, 1984)

Pedgley, D.E., *Mountain Weather* (Cicerone Press, 1979)

Steel, P., *Medical Handbook for Mountaineers* (Constable, 1988)

The Scottish Landowners' Federation and the Mountaineering Council of Scotland, *Heading for the Scottish Hills* (Scottish Landowners' Federation and Mountaineering Council of Scotland, 1990)

Useful Addresses

Glenmore Lodge (Scottish Sports Council's National Mountaineering Centre), Aviemore, Inverness-shire PH22 1QU (0479 86 256).

The John Muir Trust (Membership Secretary), Keith Anderson, FREEPOST, John Muir Trust, Edinburgh EH9 0LX (031 667 9272).

Mountaincall Weather 24-hour Forecast 0898 500 442 (East) 0898 500 441 (West).

The Mountaineering Council for Scotland, 12 Douglas Crescent, Edinburgh EH12 5BB.

The National Trust for Scotland (Headquarters), 5 Charlotte Square, Edinburgh EH2 4DU (031 226 5922).

The Scottish Landowners' Federation, 18 Abercromby Place, Edinburgh EH3 6TY (031 556 4466).

The Scottish Rights of Way Society, Unit 2, John Cotton Business Centre, 172 Easter Road, Edinburgh EH7 5RA (031 652 2937).

The Scottish Youth Hostels Association, District Office, 161 Warrender Park Road, Edinburgh EH9 1EQ (031 229 8660).

Index

Where it differs from the spelling on the map used, the Gaelic spelling is given, followed by a translated meaning.